Letts

BRAND NEW

CM01603317

KS3

VISUAL REVISION GUIDE

SUCCESS

QUESTIONS & ANSWERS

ENGLISH

Level 4–7

Kath Jordan

ANSWER BOOK

Pages 8–9

A 1 d); 2 b); 3 a); 4 c); 5 b).

B 1 Sample answers include: 'Kingshaw got up and flapped his arms' – he doesn't like the crow, it makes him uneasy and he wants it to go away 'Stupid to be scared . . . bird do?' – he is angry with himself for being frightened **(4 marks for 2 examples and explanations)**

2 a) They are very short. b) It creates tension, fear and a feeling of breathlessness. **(3 marks)**

C Marks will be awarded as follows: **1–2 (below level 4)** marks for a simple, generalised comment which relates to just one bullet point or repeats the prompts. **3–4 marks (level 4)** for an answer which supports general comment about one bullet point with detail from the text. **5–6 marks (level 5)** for an answer which supports general comment with detail from the text and addresses all bullet points. **7–8 marks (level 6)** for an answer which addresses all of the bullet points, making specific comments supported by explanation and a range of detail from the text. **9–10 marks (level 7)** for an answer which does all of the above, focusing on aspects of language and or structure and giving a personal response.

Pages 12–13

A 1 b); 2 a); 3 c); 4 d); 5 a).

B 1 a) *it, she/her* **(2 marks)**

b) Sample answers include: it makes Catherine Linton seem inhuman and it shows that the narrator doesn't feel any sympathy for her. **(2 marks for 2 correct points)**

2 Atmosphere: frightening and ghostly. **(1 mark)** Words and phrases: sample answers include 'ice-cold hand', 'horror of nightmare', 'terror and doleful cry'. **(2 marks for 4 words/phrases from the list)**

C See answers for pages 8–9 C.

Pages 16–17

A 1 a); 2 b); 3 d); 4 c); 5 b).

B 1 Exclamation and question marks **(1 mark)** indicate that they are shouting and there is a lot of disagreement. **(1 mark)**

2 Because Billy is so thin and dirty, he looks like a Jewish child from a concentration camp; the Jews were gassed in mass showers and Billy is running towards the shower; Billy resembles a Jew, so the bully, Mr Sugden, is compared to a Nazi. **(2 marks)**

3 Sample answers include: The phrases 'hands closed into fists and lashed his body around' **(1 mark for 2 words or phrases)** describe violent actions and make him seem like a boxer. **(2 marks for two points)**

C See answers for pages 8–9 C.

Pages 20–21

A 1 c); 2 c); 3 d); 4 c); 5 b).

B 1 Sample answers include: 'All year', 'daily' – the boy knows the place well, visits it regularly, understands how the place changes; 'every spring' – the boy follows the same pattern each year, it is like a ritual. **(4 marks for 2 examples and 2 explanations)**

2 Sample answers include: emphasises his terror and shows that the boy is certain that something bad will happen. **(2 marks for 2 comments)**

3 5, 2, 1, 4, 3 **(1 mark)**

C See answers for pages 8–9 C.

Pages 22–23

A 1 d); 2 b); 3 c); 4 b); 5 d).

B 1 Sample answers include: 'hard as a knot' – makes you think of the texture of rope, the berries would be unpleasant and difficult to eat; 'palms sticky as Bluebeard's' – the children imagine that the juice is like blood on their hands, like the famous pirate Bluebeard, which shows that collecting the blackberries is an exciting adventure. **(4 marks for 2 similes and explanations)**

2 'hoarded' and 'cache', the image is of pirates storing their treasure, the berries are precious to the boy, collecting the berries is an exciting adventure, the boys might play a game like 'pirates'. **(3 marks for 2 words and explanation).**

C See answers for pages 8–9 C.

Pages 24–25

A 1 c); 2 a); 3 d); 4 b); 5 d).

B 1 'Long' – excitement and anticipation; 'short' – fear and disappointment. **(2 marks)**

2 'Death of a Naturalist': 'bubbles gargled delicately' – this represents the sound made and shows that the poet is romanticising his childhood experience. 'Blackberry Picking': 'like thickened wine' – it describes the taste, colour and texture of the juice, it allows an adult reader to enjoy the sensory image the poet has created, again it shows that he is romanticising his experience. **(4 marks)**

3 Sample answers include: they are both about childhood experience, both begin with excitement and adventure and end with disappointment and fear, and both use adult imagery to describe childhood experience. **(1 mark for 3 points)**

C See answers for pages 8–9 C.

Pages 28–29

A 1 d); 2 b); 3 a); 4 c); 5 c).

B 1 Mealtimes; emphasises discrimination in the system; 'whereas, our mealies were served straight' [other food quotations are acceptable]. **(3 marks)**

2 Sample answers include: Temporal connective: 'After inspection', 'At lunch', 'Precisely at 4.30'. Focus on individuals etc: 'the guards would yell', 'We were required to', 'common-law prisoners used to' **(2 marks for 1 example from each list)**

3 Sample answers include: 'Val in! Val in!' – the English is given in brackets; *phuzamandla* – an explanation is given after the word 'which means…'. **(2 marks for 1 example and explanation)**

C See answers for pages 8–9 C.

Pages 32–33

A 1 b); 2 b); 3 c); 4 b); 5 d).

B 1 Uses technical vocabulary; refers to specialist equipment the reader is expected to own. **(2 marks)**

2 1) Recording from tape or vinyl to your PC
2) changing or restoring the sound on your computer
3) recording the sound onto CD.
(1 mark for each stage)

3 Sample answers include: Logical: 'for instance', 'however', 'although this can be'; Temporal: 'first of all', 'before you get stuck in'. **(2 marks for 1 example from each list)**

4 Could. **(1 mark)**

C See answers for pages 8–9 C.

Pages 36–37

A 1 c); 2 b); 3 d); 4 b); 5 c).

B 1 Sample answers include: 'in fact', 'to my mind', 'in my opinion'. **(1 mark for 2 from list)**

2 Rhetorical question – it raises questions in the reader's mind and makes them think for themselves about their own response. **(2 marks)**

3 Sample answers include: adolescent obesity – lack of exercise; poor emotional and communication development – miss out on playing games, listening to stories and interacting with other children. **(4 marks for 2 examples and explanations)**

C 1 Sample answers include: Freedom; freedom and liberty are central themes, this is what he wants for all people; King believed that all people should have freedom of speech, movement, etc. 'I' and 'we'; repeated use of 'I' indicates strong personal belief; 'we' and 'our' indicates that it is a shared version. **(4 marks 2 examples and explanations)**

2 Marks will be awarded as follows: **1–2 marks (below Level 4)** for a simple, generalised comment which relates to just one bullet point or repeats the prompts; **3 marks (Level 4)** for an answer which supports general comment about one bullet point detail from the text; **4 marks (Level 5)** for an answer which supports general comment with detail from the text addresses all bullet points; **5 marks (Level 6)** for an answer which addresses all of the bullet points, making specific comments supported by explanation and a range of detail from the text; **6 marks (Level 7)** for an answer which does all of the above, focusing on aspects of language and or structure and giving a personal response.

Pages 40–41

A 1 c); 2 c); 3 b); 4 d); 5 a).

B 1 Imperative, this section is giving instructions and recipes, it tells you what to do rather than making suggestions. **(2 marks)**

2 Sample answers include: pictures – make the leaflet look bright and inviting, shows examples of how you can present food; headings – break up the text and draw attention to important points; bullet points – get the information across in a quick and simple manner. **(2 marks for 2 examples and explanations)**

3 'Take 5!' is a familiar expression that the readers will recognise. This will make them feel secure; it is connected with relaxation so the reader will make positive connections; one aim of the leaflet is to persuade people to eat 5 pieces of fruit or vegetables every day – the title is an instruction to 'take 5' servings of fruit or vegetables. **(3 marks for 3 reasons)**

C See answers for pages 8–9 C.

Pages 42–43

A 1 d); 2 c); 3 false; 4 true; 5 d).

C The following mark scheme should be used to assess your writing.

A: Vocabulary

A1 A linked range of nouns and adjectives are used with little variation for effect. The writing relies on grammatical function words – pronouns, prepositions and determiners – rather than words that carry precise meaning. This leads to a lack of precision in the writing. **(1 mark)**

A2 Vocabulary is chosen to interest the reader and create some effects. A range of nouns and verbs is chosen for precise meaning. Adjectives and adverbs are used to add detail to the descriptions. **(2 marks)**

A3 Vocabulary is creative and arouses the reader's interest. Where it is appropriate, abstract nouns and some non-finite verbs are used to add interest. Adjectives are used to compare and contrast subject nouns. Adverbs are used to define the circumstances surrounding actions, thoughts and relationships between ideas. **(3 marks)**

A4 A range of inventive and creative vocabulary is used to engage the reader's interest. Meanings are extended using a variety of devices such as allusion, play on words, repetition, etc. **(4 marks)**

B: Sentence structure/punctuation and paragraph organisation

B1 Sentences are mainly simple or compound. Parts of sentences and ideas are mostly linked by conjunctions (e.g. and, then). Full stops and capital letters are used with accuracy. Paragraphs may show obvious divisions, as given in task. **(1–2 marks)**

B2 Sentences are varied through the use of relative clauses (e.g. who, which). Pronouns are generally used consistently as are tenses. Paragraphs are used appropriately with some sequencing and ordering of detail. **(3–4 marks)**

B3 Compound and complex sentences are used, with phrases and clauses being used to build up relevant detail. Qualifying words (e.g. 'completely') are used to convey precise meaning. Pronouns and tenses are used consistently. Punctuation is used correctly. Paragraphs are used appropriately with sequencing of detail. **(5–6 marks)**

B4 A range of grammatical structures (such as adverbials) is used to vary the focus of sentences. A range of punctuation is used correctly; sometimes to create effects. Paragraphs are varied in structure and length in order to reflect the content of the writing. **(7–8 marks)**

C: Composition and effect

C1 The description shows some awareness of the reader. Simple devices such as repetition are used to signal key features of person/object described. Although there is relevant content, there is uneven coverage of the prompts given in the question. **(1–2 marks)**

C2 The description makes attempts to engage the reader's interest. Some stylistic devices are used to reinforce the meaning of the piece, such as patterning. The topic is covered adequately, but the description is unimaginative and formulaic. **(3–4 marks)**

C3 The writing engages the reader's interest. There is a secure sense of purpose in the description. The setting is developed, and various devices are used to communicate meaning. A coherent viewpoint is presented via reflection on the description and narrative. **(5–6 marks)**

C4 The description is well written and convincing throughout. The writing engages the reader's interest. A full range of appropriate details and ideas is included. The viewpoint of the writer is consistently maintained. There is a good balance between description, information and explanation in the piece of writing. **(7–8 marks)**

Pages 44–45

A 1 c); 2 a); 3 b); 4 false; 5 false.

C The following mark scheme should be used to assess your writing.

A: Sentence structure and punctuation

Al Ideas and sentences are mostly linked using conjunctions such as 'and', 'but' and 'when'. Sentences are mainly compound, and within them sentence subjects and verbs are frequently repeated. Full stops, capital letters, question marks and exclamation marks are used to demarcate sentences, mostly accurately. **(1 mark)**

A2 Sentences are varied; relative clauses, such as those using 'who' and 'which' are used. Subordinating conjunctions, such as 'if' and 'because', develop reasons and emphasis. Commas are used within sentences, mainly with accuracy. **(2 marks)**

A3 Compound and complex sentences are used. Phrases and clauses build up detail and give information. Suggestions are given using modal verbs such as 'can' and 'would'. A variety of punctuation is used with accuracy. Different types of sentence including exclamations, commands and questions add interest and variety. **(3 marks)**

A4 Shades of meaning are expressed through the use of a range of grammatical structures such as adverbials and impersonal openings. A range of punctuation is used with accuracy; this is sometimes used to create deliberate effects, such as bullets, parentheses, etc. **(4 marks)**

A5 Sentence structure is varied as appropriate. Simple sentences are used effectively and contrasts achieve particular effects or emphasis (e.g. past/present tense and active/passive voice). Punctuation is used with accuracy to clarify meaning, avoid ambiguity and vary pace. **(5 marks)**

B: Paragraph organisation and textual cohesion

Bl Ideas are linked mainly through topic. Points may be listed in no particular order of importance. Paragraphs may be used to show obvious divisions. **(1 mark)**

B2 Paragraphs generally open with the main idea and contain examples or illustrations. **(2 marks)**

B3 Paragraphs are logically sequenced. There is a sense of introduction and conclusion. Paragraphs of different lengths are used to emphasise ideas used for persuasion or to create feelings of tension or excitement. Speech is paragraphed correctly. **(3 marks)**

B4 Detailed content is organised well within and between paragraphs. Some connectives are used to show logical relationships ('on the other hand ...'). The introduction and conclusion to persuasion and argument contribute to the persuasiveness of the text. The structure of narrative writing is controlled through paragraph length and organization. **(4 marks)**

B5 Paragraphs are varied in length to help control ideas. Cohesion of the text is reinforced by the use of a range of linking devices (adverbials, connectives). Paragraph structure is varied to create impact and develop ideas. **(5 marks)**

C: Composition and effect

C1 The given form of the writing shows some awareness of the reader. There is some relevant content but possibly uneven coverage. **(1–3 marks)**

C2 Writing is generally lively and attempts to interest the reader. A sense of purpose is shown in the content of persuasive writing and some reasons are given for ideas and opinions. In narrative writing the plot structure is clear and is balanced with some description. **(4–6 marks)**

C3 Writing is detailed and gives clear reasons for opinions. It engages the reader's interest. A range of imaginative vocabulary is used to describe people and objects. **(7–9 marks)**

C4 In persuasion and argument a range of persuasive devices are used such as repetition, humour and a consideration of the reader's needs and position. The writer's viewpoint is maintained with consistency. In narrative writing imagery is used in description and alternative narrative structures are explored. **(10–12 marks)**

C5 The tone and content of writing is appropriate and well judged. Writing seeks and achieves deliberate interaction with the reader. Narrative writing shows control and development of characters and settings. **(13–15 marks)**

D: Spelling

D1 Simple words are usually accurate. **(1 mark)**

D2 Simple and polysyllabic words are generally accurate. **(2 marks)**

D3 Words with complex but regular patterns are generally accurate. **(3 marks)**

D4 Most spelling, including irregular words, is accurate. **(4 marks)**

D5 Virtually all spelling, including complex irregular words, is correct. **(5 marks)**

Pages 46–47

A 1 false; 2 b); 3 c); 4 b); 5 a).

C See answers for pages 44–45.

Pages 48–49

A 1 false; 2 true; 3 d); 4 c); 5 b).

C See answers for pages 42–43.

Pages 50–51

A 1 b); 2 true; 3 b); 4 d); 5 true.

C See answers for pages 42-43.

Pages 56–57

A 1 b); 2 c); 3 a); 4 c); 5 b).

B 1 He compares love to the sea swallowing everything up, it shows that he thinks love makes all other experiences valueless. **(2 marks)**

2 He compares his desires to hunting dogs tearing his heart (the hart) apart, he thinks love is painful and causes suffering, he says that his desires will never leave his heart alone. **(3 marks for comparison and explanation)**

3 She will stay indoors for seven years, walk around wearing a veil and crying to mourn for her dead brother. **(2 marks for complete explanation)**

C See answers for pages 8-9 C.

Pages 58–59

A 1 b); 2 c); 3 d); 4 a); 5 b).

B 1 Bear baiting, **(1 mark)** 'the stake, baited, unmuzzled'. **(1 mark)**

2 Monosyllabic [one syllable or short are also acceptable] **(1 mark)** keeps the exchange moving at a fast pace. **(1 mark)**

3 She means that although Olivia thinks Viola is a man, she is actually a woman **(1 mark)** The audience would appreciate the dramatic irony – they know that Olivia is mistaken; they would find it particularly amusing because they would be watching a boy, playing a woman, playing a man. **(2 marks – 1 for each part of explanation)**

C See answers for pages 8–9 C.

Pages 64–65

A 1 b); 2 a); 3 c); 4 d); 5 a).

B 1 Sample answers include: they are kinsmen – you shouldn't kill your relatives; he is Duncan's subject – you should be loyal to your king; he is Duncan's host – you should protect guests in your house. **(4 marks for 2 reasons and explanations)**

2 Sample answers include: 'his surcease', 'this blow', 'bear the knife', 'taking-off', 'the horrid deed' **(1 mark for 2 euphemisms)** He uses euphemisms because he knows what he is planning is wrong, he can't face what he's about to do so he can't bring himself to say it. **(2 marks)**

C See answers for pages 8–9 C.

Pages 66–67

A 1 c); 2 b); 3 d); 4 b); 5 b).

B 1 Frothy waves will swallow up ships, cornfields will be flattened, trees will be blown down, castles, pyramids and palaces will collapse. **(2 marks for 2 consequences)**

2 He begins by saying 'I conjure you'. This sounds like the beginning of a spell, he starts speaking in rhyming couplets like the witches and the apparitions, he uses more language to do with destruction in this scene. **(1 mark for each reason)**

3 He believes that the trees will never uproot themselves and move towards his castle and that he is invincible. **(2 marks)**

C See answers for pages 8–9 C.

Pages 72–73

A 1 b); 2 a); 3 d); 4 d); 5 b).

B 1 Using so many adjectives emphasises how bad Scroop has been, makes his betrayal seem worse, makes him appear to be a monster. **(1 mark for 1 reason from the list)**

2 Repetition – emphasises all the ways that Scroop has betrayed and deceived the king; rhetorical questions – shows how upset the king is because he questions how he could have been so deceived, the answer to each question is always the same. **(4 marks for 2 devices and explanations)**

3 Compares Scroop's betrayal to Adam and Eve's sin which led to them being exiled from the Garden of Eden; this is know as the original sin and is considered to be the root of all evil; in comparing it to the fall of man the king is saying that this is the worst thing that could possibly happen. **(2 marks)**

C See answers for pages 8–9 C.

Pages 74–75

A 1 c); 2 c); 3 a); 4 a); 5 b).

B 1 He wants to encourage them and make them feel that they are equal and important to him. **(1 mark)**

2 Sample answers include: 'imitate', 'stiffen', 'set', 'stretch'; he is instructing and ordering them to go into battle. **(2 marks)**

3 Sample answers include: he wants to inspire feelings of loyalty, to inspire them to defend their country and prove their worth to their families. **(2 marks for 2 reasons)**

4 Sample answers include: 'eye … like the brass cannon' – he compares the soldiers eyes to weapons to continue the war theme; 'like greyhounds in the slips' – he uses this to describe the soldiers as eager to start the hunt for the game. The enemy is being compared to the hare that the dogs would chase and kill. **(2 marks for 1 simile and explanation)**

C See answers for pages 8–9 C.

Pages 76–77

A 1 c); 2 d); 3 b); 4 c); 5 b).

B 1 Accommodation, committed, strawberries, separate, definite, churches, leaves, possible, successful, beautiful. **(1 mark for each)**

2 Monkeys, boys **(1 mark)** factories, babies, tries. **(1 mark)**

3 If a word ends in a vowel and then y, just add an s. If a word ends in a consonant and y, change the y to an i and add es. **(1 mark)**

C 1 quickly, socks, which, stepped, ankles, pigmentation, were, ancient, **(1 mark for each correct answer)**

2 There, through, We're, saw, sore, know, hear, knot. **(1 mark for each correct answer)**

Pages 78–79

A 1 d); 2 c); 3 c); 4 c); 5 a).

B 1 I went to the shop and (I) bought a chocolate bar. [The use of *I* in the second clause is optional]. **(1 mark)**

2 Due to track repairs, the trains were late. **(1 mark for moving the clause, 1 mark for correct punctuation)**

3 The teacher, filled with despair, marked the exam papers. **(1 mark for embedding the clause, 1 marks for correct punctuation)**

4 Don't, who's (who is), couldn't, doesn't, Joanne's bag, the girls' bags (plural), the girl's bag, the poet's writing. **(1 mark for each)**

C 1 a time, topic, talk. 1b 'I took a train . . . rubbish bags'; 'In another bout . . . Liverpool specializes'; 'And so . . . '**(1 mark for each correct answer)**

2 a) When the rope snapped, the climber, who was very frightened, fell and broke his leg.

b) 'Can I go out tonight Mum?' asked Alison.

c) When the alarm rang, the workers left the building calmly.

d) 'Gosh!' exclaimed the woman. 'I didn't see you there.' **(2 marks for each correct answer)**

Mock SAT Paper One
Reading, pages 81–91

1 Scrap of beef: feeds it to the hawk; swivel: attaches it to the jesses; leash: feeds it through the swivel or ties it around his glove. **(1 mark for complete answer)**

2 Hang upside down from the glove. **(1 mark)**

3 Sample answers include: he approaches slowly – this shows that he knows how to move without frightening the hawk; he chants her name softly – this shows he knows how to calm her down; he attaches the leash and ties it around his finger – he knows how to use the leash and jesses and he understands the importance of keeping everything secure so that the hawk cannot fly away. **(4 marks for 2 examples and explanations)**

4 He isn't sure whether Billy is joking or being serious; he wants Billy to think that he understands it's a joke and that he isn't scared. **(2 marks)**

5 **1 mark** for a simple, generalised comment which relates to just one bullet point or repeats the prompts;
2 marks for an answer which supports general comment about one bullet point with detail from the text;
3 marks for an answer which supports general comment with detail from the text and addresses all bullet points;
4 marks for an answer which addresses all of the bullet points, making specific comments supported by explanation and a range of detail from the text;

5–6 marks for an answer which does all of the above, focusing on aspects of language and or structure and giving a personal response.

6 See answer to **question 5**.

7 Sample answers include: 'the reef gradually dipped . . .' – the underwater landscape invites the diver to move slowly, the use of the word gradually suggests slow movement; 'its edges were rippling softly' – a ripple is a very slight movement of water and used with the word softly this makes you think that the movement must be slow otherwise waves would be created. **(2 marks for 1 example and explanation)**

8 It suggests that he is amazed and can hardly believe what he is seeing; 'transfixed' suggests that he is unable to move because he finds that experience so unexpected and unusual; 'realisation' suggests that he didn't know immediately what he was looking at. **(2 marks for 2 points from the list)**

9 'single most . . . in my life' – he is full of admiration, by suggesting that he has never seen anything more beautiful he emphasises its beauty; 'Some people . . . fluid and benign' – he wants to defend it from the cruel things other people have said, the range of adjectives he uses shows how incredible he thinks it is. **(4 marks)**

10 He is sorry to have had such a short time to look at the creature and believes he will never see it again but is thrilled and delighted to have seen it at all. **(2 marks)**.

11 Sample answers include: at first he can only see a shadow moving above him – he doesn't know what it is; he describes himself as unprepared – this tells the reader that what happens next will be unusual or exciting; 'soared', 'rollercoaster' and 'sped off' create a feeling of speed, this is exciting because the manta ray seemed to be slow and gentle earlier. **(4 marks for a full answer)**

12 See answer to **question 5**.

13 To persuade people to give money; it gives examples of what your money can do; it gives information about what the charity does; it shows animals that have been helped by the charity. **(3 marks for purpose and 2 reasons)**

14 Somebody actually spoke those words; it makes the story more believable if somebody who was involved speaks about it. **(2 marks)**

15 'Just' and 'small' make the donation sound manageable for everybody; 'cruelty' is a powerful and persuasive word; the final phrase is very close to the name of the charity. **(2 marks)**

16 See answer to **question 5**.

Writing, page 92

See answer for pages 44–45.

Mock SAT Paper Two Shakespeare Reading, page 94

Level 3 (1–3 marks)
A simple retelling of the scenes. No reference to the text.

Level 4 (4–10 marks)
A few simple comments about the characters. Answer focuses on retelling the scenes. Some reference to the text but no supporting explanation.

Level 5 (11–17 marks)
Answer contains a straightforward commentary on the scenes. Displays a good level of understanding of characters and their motivation. Comments are supported by reference to the text.

Level 6 (18–23 marks)
A focused answer with a degree of exploration of the text. Detailed commentary displays understanding of characters, motivation and relationships. There is some awareness of language used and how this contributes to character and atmosphere. References to the text are appropriate and relevant.

Level 7 (24–30 marks)
A full answer showing knowledge of the text and the characters and focusing on the requirements of the question. The answer shows a good understanding of how language contributes to the exploration of characters, motivation, relationships and themes. The answer shows insight and gives some personal response. Comments are justified by carefully selected references to the text.

Writing, page 95

See answer for pages 42–43.

LETTS EDUCATIONAL
The Chiswick Centre
414 Chiswick High Road
London W4 5TF
Tel: 020 8996 3333
Fax: 020 8742 8390
Email: mail@lettsed.co.uk
Website: www.letts-education.com

ISBN 1-84085-952-0
9 781840 859522

Letts

BRAND NEW

KS3

VISUAL REVISION GUIDE

SUCCESS

QUESTIONS & ANSWERS

QUESTIONS & ANSWERS

ENGLISH

Level 4–7

Kath Jordan

CONTENTS

Homework Diary

TOPIC	SCORE
Post-1914 fiction	/22
Pre-1914 fiction	/22
Comparing texts	/22
'Death of a Naturalist'	/22
'Blackberry Picking'	/22
Comparing two poems	/22
Autobiography/recount	/22
Information and explanation	/22
Persuasion and argument	/22
Media text	/22
Writing to describe	/25
Writing to imagine, explore, entertain	/35
Writing to argue and persuade	/35
Writing to inform and explain	/25
Writing to review, analyse, comment	/25
Twelfth Night	/22
Macbeth	/22
Henry V	/22
Spelling	/32
Punctuation and grammar	/32

Progress Plotter

Once you have completed a unit, and filled in your score on the Homework Diary opposite, use this Progress Plotter to chart your success! Fill in the boxes with your score for each unit and watch your results get better and better.

Scores and Levels

Use this rough guide to convert your total scores for each topic into a National Curriculum level.

Reading and Shakespeare (../22)

3–6 marks	level 3
7–10 marks	level 4
11–14 marks	level 5
15–18 marks	level 6
19–22 marks	level 7

Writing (../20)

1–5 marks	level 3
6–10 marks	level 4
11–14 marks	level 5
15–18 marks	level 6
19–20 marks	level 7

Writing (../30)

5–9 marks	level 3
10–14 marks	level 4
15–19 marks	level 5
20–24 marks	level 6
25–30 marks	level 7

Post-1914 fiction				
Pre-1914 fiction				
Comparing texts				
'Death of a Naturalist'				
'Blackberry Picking'				
Comparing two poems				
Autobiography/recount				
Information and explanation				
Persuasion and argument				
Media text				
Writing to describe				
Writing to imagine, explore, entertain				
Writing to argue and persuade				
Writing to review, analyse, comment				
Twelfth Night				
Macbeth				
Henry V				
Spelling				
Punctuation and grammar				
	Nearly all right – excellent work!	*More than half* – good – but keep trying	*Less than half* – Room for improvement	*Under 5* – needs more work

POST-1914 FICTION

In this extract, the young boy, Kingshaw has gone for a walk to escape the bully he and his mother are staying with. In the isolated cornfields some way from the house, he has a terrifying experience when he is chased by an unexpected predator.

Read the extract carefully and answer the questions that follow.

When he first saw the crow he took no notice. There had been several crows. This one glided into the corn on its enormous, ragged black wings. He began to be aware of it when it rose up suddenly, circled overhead, and then dived, to land not very far away from him. Kingshaw could see the feathers on its head, shining black in between the butter-coloured cornstalks. Then it rose, and circled, and came down again, this time not quite landing, but flapping about his head, beating its wings and making a sound like flat leather pieces being slapped together. It was the largest crow he had ever seen. As it came down for the third time, he looked up and noticed its beak, opening in a screech. The inside of its mouth was scarlet, it had small glinting eyes.

Kingshaw got up and flapped his arms. For a moment, the bird retreated a little way off, and higher up in the sky. He began to walk rather quickly back, through the path in the corn, looking ahead of him. Stupid to be scared of a rotten bird. What could a bird do? But he felt his own extreme isolation, high up in the cornfield.

For a moment, he could only hear the soft thudding of his own footsteps, and the silky sound of the corn, brushing against him. Then there was a rush of air, as the great crow came beating down, and wheeled about his head. The beak opened and the hoarse caw came out again and again, from inside the scarlet mouth.

Kingshaw began to run, not caring now, if he trampled the corn, wanting to get away, down into the next field. He thought that the corn might be some kind of crow's food store, in which he was seen as an invader. Perhaps this was only the first of a whole battalion of crows, that would rise up and swoop at him. Get on the grass then, he thought, get on to the grass, that'll be safe, it'll go away. He wondered if it had mistaken him for some hostile animal, lurking down in the corn.

His progress was very slow, through the cornfield, the thick stalks bunched together and got in his way, and he had to shove them back with his arms. But he reached the gate and climbed it, and dropped on to the grass of the field on the other side. Sweat was running down his forehead and into his eyes. He looked up. The crow kept on coming. He ran.

But it wasn't easy to run down this field, either, because of the tractor ruts. He began to leap wildly from side to side of them, his legs stretched as far as they could go, and for a short time, it seemed that he did go faster. The crow dived again, and, as it rose, Kingshaw felt the tip of its black wing, beating against his face. He gave a sudden, dry sob. Then his left foot caught in one of the ruts and he keeled over, going down straight forwards.

He lay with his face in the coarse grass, panting and sobbing by turns, with the sound of his own blood pumping through his ears. He felt the sun on the back of his neck, and his ankle was wrenched. But he would be able to get up. He raised his head, and wiped two fingers across his face. A streak of blood came off, from where a thistle had scratched him. He got unsteadily to his feet, taking in deep, desperate breaths of the close air. He could not see the crow.

But when he began to walk forwards again, it rose up from the grass a little way off, and began to circle and swoop. Kingshaw broke into a run, sobbing and wiping the damp mess of tears and sweat off his face with one hand. There was a blister on his ankle, rubbed raw by the sandal strap. The crow was still quite high, soaring easily, to keep pace with him. Now, he had scrambled over the third gate, and he was in the field next to the one that belonged to Warings. He could see the back of the house, he began to run much faster.

This time, he fell and lay completely winded. Through the runnels of sweat and the sticky tufts of his own hair, he could see a figure looking down at him from one of the top windows of the house.

Then, there was a single screech, and the terrible beating of wings, and the crow swooped down and landed in the middle of his back.

Kingshaw thought that, in the end, it must have been his screaming that frightened it off, for he dared not move. He lay and closed his eyes and felt the claws of the bird, digging into his skin, through the thin shirt, and began to scream in a queer, gasping sort of way. After a moment or two, the bird rose. He had expected it to begin pecking at him with its beak, remembering terrible stories about vultures that went for living people's eyes. He could not believe in his own escape.

From *I'm the King of the Castle*
by Susan Hill

A Choose just one answer, a, b, c or d.

1 Kingshaw is frightened because
a) he is lost in a cornfield
b) he is lost in a forest
c) he is being chased by a vulture
d) he is being chased by a crow

2 '... a sound like flat pieces of leather being slapped together' is
a) a metaphor
b) a simile
c) personification
d) onomatopoeia

3 Kingshaw found it difficult to run in the cornfield because
a) the corn stalks got in the way
b) it was very muddy
c) he had sprained his ankle
d) the tractor ruts were too deep

4 The bird hurt Kingshaw by
a) landing on his head
b) pecking at his eyes
c) digging its claws in his back
d) knocking him to the ground

5 Kingshaw escaped because
a) he ran away
b) the bird flew away
c) he chased the bird away
d) his friend saved him

Score .... /5

B Answer all parts of all questions.

1 Look at the section 'Kingshaw got up and flapped his arms' to 'lurking down in the corn'.

From this section, how do we know what Kingshaw is feeling?

Give **two** examples of what he thinks or does and explain how this shows what he is feeling.

Example: ....

Explanation: ....

....

Example: ....

Explanation: ....

.... 4 marks

2 Look at the paragraph beginning 'His progress was very slow'.

a) What do you notice about the sentences at the end of this paragraph?

.... 1 mark

b) What is the effect of this?

....

.... 2 marks

Score .... /7

C **This is a SATs-style question. Your answer should respond to each of the bullet points.**

1 **How does the writer of this passage build increasing tension through this text?**

You should write about:

- the setting
- the structure of the text
- the way the character reacts to his situation.

10 marks

Score .... /10

TOTAL SCORE /22

For more help on this topic see KS3 English Success Guide pages 10–15

PRE-1914 FICTION

In this extract, the narrator, Mr Lockwood is visiting Wuthering Heights. Bad weather and heavy snowfall across the Yorkshire Moors prevent him from leaving for home. Mr Heathcliffe, the ill-tempered owner of Wuthering Heights, is reluctant to allow Lockwood to stay for the night but a servant takes pity on him and shows him upstairs. He finds a disused room with a large oak bed next to a window ledge and decides to sleep there. That night he is unable to sleep as he is plagued by bad dreams and noises outside the window.

This text was written in the 19th century so you may find some of the language difficult and unfamiliar. A glossary is provided at the end of the extract to help you with some of the unfamiliar vocabulary.

Read the extract carefully and answer the questions that follow.

This time, I remembered I was lying in the oak closet, and I heard distinctly the gusty wind, and the driving snow; I heard also, the fir-bough repeat its teasing sound, and ascribed it to the right cause: but it annoyed me so much, that I resolved to silence it, if possible; and, I thought, I rose and endeavoured to unhasp the casement. The hook was soldered into the staple: a circumstance observed by me when awake, but forgotten.

'I must stop it, nevertheless!' I muttered, knocking my knuckles through the glass, and stretching an arm out to seize the importunate branch: instead of which, my fingers closed on the fingers of a little, ice-cold hand!

The intense horror of nightmare came over me; I tried to draw back my arm, but the hand clung to it, and a most melancholy voice sobbed,

'Let me in — let me in!'

'Who are you?' I asked, struggling, meanwhile, to disengage myself.

'Catherine Linton,' it replied. 'I'm come home: I'd lost my way on the moor!' As it spoke, I discerned, obscurely, a child's face looking through the window.

Terror made me cruel; and, finding it useless to attempt shaking the creature off, I pulled its wrist on to the broken pane, and rubbed it to and fro till blood ran down and soaked the bed-clothes: still it wailed, 'Let me in!' and maintained its tenacious grip, almost maddening me with fear.

'How can I?' I said at length. 'Let <u>me</u> go, if you want me to let you in!'

The fingers relaxed, I snatched mine through the hole, hurriedly piled the books up in a pyramid against it, and stopped my ears to exclude the lamentable prayer.

I seemed to keep them closed above a quarter of an hour, yet, the instant I listened again, there was the doleful cry moaning on!

'Begone!' I shouted, 'I'll never let you in, not if you beg for twenty years!'

'It's twenty years,' mourned the voice, 'twenty years, I've been a waif for twenty years!'

From *Wuthering Heights*
by Emily Brontë (1818–1848)

Glossary

ascribed	put it down to
unhasp	unhook
casement	window
importunate	persistent/annoying
discerned, obscurely	saw but not clearly
tenacious	stubborn/firm

A Choose just one answer, a, b, c or d.

1 The sentence type most often used in the dialogue (conversation) is
a) interrogative
b) exclamatory
c) directive (imperative)
d) declarative

2 The narrative perspective in this text is
a) 1st person
b) 2nd person
c) 3rd person
d) omniscient

3 At first the narrator believes the noise that wakes him is
a) a child
b) a bad dream
c) a tree branch tapping on the window
d) a ghost

4 The words *he, she, it* are
a) nouns
b) verbs
c) adverbs
d) pronouns

5 Which of the following words is <u>not</u> a synonym (alternative) for *lamentable*?
a) laudable
b) sorrowful
c) sad
d) woeful

Score .... /5

B Answer all parts of all questions.

1 Look again at the section beginning '"Who are you?" I asked'.

a) Which pronoun does the author use to write about Catherine Linton and which pronoun would you expect the author to use?

Pronoun used: ....

Pronoun expected: .... 2 marks

b) What effect does the author's choice of pronoun have?

....

.... 2 marks

2 How would you describe the atmosphere of this text? List four words or phrases that help to create this atmosphere.

Atmosphere: .... 1 mark

Words and phrases: ....

.... 2 marks

Score .... /7

C

This is a SATs-style question. Your answer should respond to each of the bullet points.

1 **Does the narrator show any sympathy towards Catherine Linton?**

You should write about:

- the language he uses to describe her
- what he says to her
- the way he behaves.

....

....

....

....

....

....

....

....

....

.... 5 marks

2 **How does the author create a feeling of fear and horror in this passage?**

You should write about:

- the way the setting is described
- the language used in the extract
- the way the narrator behaves.

....

....

....

....

....

....

....

....

....

.... 5 marks

Score .... /10

TOTAL SCORE /22

For more help on this topic see KS3 English Success Guide pages 10–15

COMPARING TEXTS

In this extract Mr Sugden, the PE teacher, punishes Billy for playing badly in a football match by making him take a cold shower. Mr Sugden uses his authority to bully and intimidate Billy, his pupil.

Read the extract carefully and answer the questions that follow.

He undressed quickly, bending his pumps free of his heels and sliding them off without untying the laces. When he stood up the black soles of his socks stamped damp imprints on the dry floor, which developed into a haphazard set of footprints when he removed his socks and stepped around pulling his jeans down. His ankles and knees were ingrained with ancient dirt which seemed to belong to the pigmentation of his skin. His left leg sported a mud stripe, and both his knees were encrusted. The surfaces of these mobile crusts were hair-lined, and with every flexion of the knee these lines opened into frown-like furrows.

For an instant, as he hurried into the showers, with one leg angled in running, with his dirty legs and huge rib cage moulding the skin of his white body, with his hollow cheek in profile, and the sabre of shadow emanating from the eye-hole, just for a moment he resembled an old print of a child hurrying towards the final solution.

***

While he worked on his ankles and heels Sugden stationed three boys at one end of the showers and moved to the other end, where the controls fed into the pipes on the wall. . . The blunt arrow was pointing to HOT. Sugden swung it back over WARM to COLD. For a few seconds there was no visible change in the temperature, and the red slice held steady, still dominating the dial. Then it began to recede, slowly at first, then swiftly, its share of the face diminishing rapidly.

The cold water made Billy gasp. He held out his hands as though testing for rain, then ran for the end. The three guards barred the exit.

'Hey up, shift! Let me out, you rotten dogs!' They held him easily so he swished back to the other end, yelling all the way along. Sugden pushed him in the chest as he clung his way round the corner.

'Got a sweat on, Casper?'

'Let me out, Sir. Let me come.'

'I thought you'd like a cooler after your exertions in goal.'

'I'm frozen!'

'Really?'

'Gi' o'er, Sir! It's not right!'

'And was it right when you let the last goal in?'

'I couldn't help it!'

'Rubbish, lad.'

Billy tried another rush. Sugden repelled it, so he tried the other end again.

Every time he tried to escape the three boys bounced him back, stinging him with their snapping towels as he retreated. He tried manoeuvring the nozzles, but whichever way he twisted them the water still found him out. Until finally he gave up, and stood amongst them, tolerating the freezing spray in silence.

From *A Kestrel for a Knave*
by Barry Hines

Glossary

final solution: in World War II, Hitler's 'final solution' was to kill millions of Jews. Many of them were killed by gassing in mass showers

In this extract George and Lennie meet Curley, the boss's son, for the first time. Curley uses his physical presence and aggression to intimidate Lennie.

Read the extract and answer the questions that follow.

His eyes passed over the new men and he stopped. He glanced coldly at George and then at Lennie. His arms gradually bent at the elbows and his hands closed into fists. He stiffened and went into a slight crouch. His glance was at once calculating and pugnacious. Lennie squirmed under the look and shifted his feet nervously. Curley stepped gingerly close to him. 'You the new guys the old man was waitin' for?'

'We just come,' said George.

'Let the big guy talk.'

Lennie twisted with embarrassment.

George said: 'S'pose he don't want to talk?'

Curley lashed his body around. 'By Christ, he's gotta talk when he's spoke to. What the hell are you gettin' into it for?'

'We travel together,' said George coldly.

'Oh, so it's that way.'

George was tense and motionless. 'Yeah, it's that way.'

Lennie was looking helplessly to George for instruction.

'An' you won't let the big guy talk, is that it?'

'He can talk if he wants to tell you anything.' He nodded slightly to Lennie.

'We jus' come in,' said Lennie softly.

Curley stared levelly at him. 'Well, nex' time you answer when you're spoke to.' He turned towards the door and walked out, and his elbows were still bent out a little.

George watched him out, and then turned back to the swamper. 'Say what the hell's he got on his shoulder? Lennie didn't do nothing to him.'

The old man looked cautiously at the door to make sure no one was listening. 'That's the boss's son,' he said quietly. 'Curley's pretty handy. He's done quite a bit in the ring. He's a lightweight, and he's handy.'

'Well let him be handy,' said George. 'He don't have to take after Lennie. Lennie didn't do nothing to him. What's he got against Lennie?'

The swamper considered: '-Well – tell you what. Curley's like a lot of little guys. He hates big guys. He's alla time picking scraps with big guys. Kind of like he's mad at 'em because he ain't a big guy. You seen little guys like that, ain't you? Always scrappy?'

'Sure,' said George. 'I seen plenty tough little guys. But this Curley better not make no mistakes about Lennie. Lennie ain't handy, but this Curley punk is gonna get hurt if he messes around with Lennie.'

From *Of Mice and Men*
by John Steinbeck

A Choose just one answer, a, b, c or d.

1 Mr Sugden was angry with Billy because
a) he let a goal in
b) he refused to have a shower
c) he bullied another pupil
d) he wouldn't join in the PE lesson

2 Another verb that means tolerate is
a) enjoy
b) endure
c) refuse
d) fight

3 Which punctuation mark is used most in the speech of Billy and Mr Sugden ?
a) comma
b) question mark
c) full stop
d) exclamation mark

4 Which verb is not used to describe Lennie's movement?
a) squirmed
b) shifted
c) shuffled
d) twisted

5 In the second extract the reader's sympathy is with
a) Curley
b) Lennie
c) George
d) the swamper

Score .... **/5**

B Answer all parts of all questions.

1 Look closely at the way the dialogue is punctuated in the first extract.
Give the two main punctuation marks used and explain what effect this has.

Punctuation: .... 1 mark

Explanation: .... 1 mark

2 Look closely at the section beginning 'For an instant...' (*A Kestrel for a Knave*)
Explain how this comparison creates sympathy for Billy.

....

....

....

.... 2 marks

3 Look closely at the section beginning 'His eyes passed over the new men...' and ending 'What the hell are you gettin' into it for?' (*Of Mice and Men*)
Give two words or phrases used to make Curley seem threatening and explain why they are effective.

Words and phrases: .... 1 mark

Explanation: ....

.... 2 marks

Score .... **/7**

C This is a SATs-style question. Your answer should respond to each of the bullet points.

1 **Compare the ways in which the two writers create sympathy for the victims of bullying and intimidation.**

You should write about:

- the way Billy and Lennie react to their situations
- the way the bullies are presented
- the way that other characters behave towards and talk about the main characters

...10 marks

Score .... /10

TOTAL SCORE /22

For more help on this topic see KS3 English Success Guide pages 10–15

READING POETRY

Read both poems and answer the questions that follow. Questions on pages 24–25 require you to compare the two poems.

Death of a Naturalist

All year the flax-dam festered in the heart
Of the townland; green and heavy headed
Flax had rotted there, weighted down by huge sods.
Daily it sweltered in the punishing sun.
Bubbles gargled delicately, bluebottles
Wove a strong gauze of sound around the smell.
There were dragon-flies, spotted butterflies,
But best of all was the warm thick slobber
Of frogspawn that grew like clotted water
In the shade of the banks. Here, every spring
I would fill jampotsful of the jellied
Specks to range on window-sills at home,
On shelves at school, and wait and watch until
The fattening dots burst into nimble-
Swimming tadpoles. Miss Walls would tell us how
The daddy frog was called a bullfrog
And how he croaked and how the mammy frog
Laid hundreds of little eggs and this was
Frogspawn.You could tell the weather by frogs too
For they were yellow in the sun and brown
In rain.

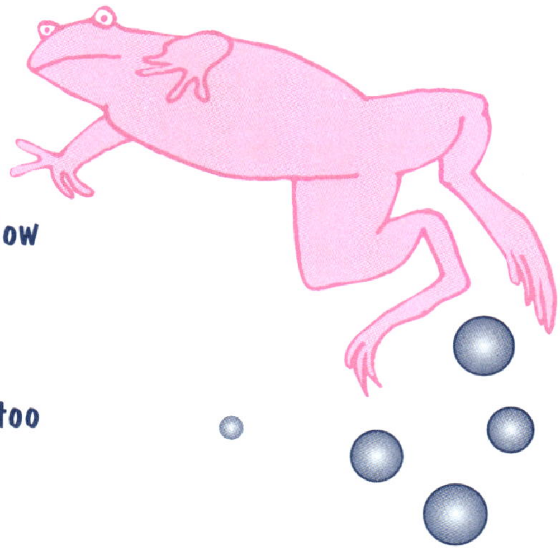

Then one hot day when fields were rank
With cowdung in the grass and angry frogs
Invaded the flax-dam; I ducked through hedges
To a coarse croaking that I had not heard
Before. The air was thick with a bass chorus.
Right down the dam gross-bellied frogs were cocked
On sods; their loose necks pulsed like sails. Some hopped:
The slap and plop were obscene threats. Some sat
Poised like mud grenades, their blunt heads farting.
I sickened, turned, and ran. The great slime kings
Were gathered there for vengeance and I knew
That if I dipped my hand the spawn would clutch it.

Seamus Heaney

Blackberry Picking

Late August, given heavy rain and sun
For a full week, the blackberries would ripen.
At first, just one, a glossy purple clot
Among others, red, green, hard as a knot.
You ate the first one and its flesh was sweet
Like thickened wine: summer's blood was in it
Leaving stains upon the tongue and lust for
Picking. Then red ones inked up and that hunger
Sent us out with milk-cans, pea-tins, jam-pots
Where briars scratched and wet grass bleached our boots.
Round hayfields, cornfields and potato-drills
We trekked and picked until the cans were full,
Until the tinkling bottom had been covered
With green ones, and on top big dark blobs burned
Like a plate of eyes. Our hands were peppered
With thorn pricks, our palms sticky as Bluebeard's.

We hoarded the fresh berries in the byre.
But when the bath was filled we found a fur,
A rat grey fungus, glutting on our cache.
The juice was stinking too. Once off the bush
The fruit fermented, the sweet flesh would turn sour.
I always felt like crying. It wasn't fair
That all the lovely canfuls smelt of rot.
Each year I hoped they would keep, knew they would not.

Seamus Heaney

Glossary

Bluebeard: a pirate who killed many of his wives by chopping off their heads
byre: a cowshed
cache: a hidden store of treasure, provisions or weapons

'DEATH OF A NATURALIST'

A Choose just one answer, a, b, c or d.

1 The poem is called 'Death of a Naturalist' because
a) a naturalist is killed
b) the boy kills the frogs
c) the boy loses his interest in nature
d) the 'great slime kings' kill the boy

2 When does the boy collect frogspawn?
a) all year
b) every day
c) every spring
d) every summer

3 'Poised like mud grenades' is
a) a metaphor
b) personification
c) an oxymoron
d) a simile

4 Which of the following techniques is not used in the poem?
a) onomatopoeia
b) simile
c) rhyme
d) alliteration

5 How many different voices can you hear in the poem?
a) one
b) two
c) three
d) four

Score .... /5

B Answer all parts of all questions.

1 The poet uses references to time to organise his poem. **Give two examples of references to time and explain why they are effective.**

Example: ....

Explanation: ....

Example: ....

Explanation: .... 4 marks

2 Look closely at the final sentence of the poem. **Explain why the poet uses the phrase 'I knew'.**

....

.... 2 marks

3 Put the events of the poem in order by numbering the following points.

.... The boy is frightened of the frogs and runs away.

.... The boy collects frogspawn every spring.

.... The boy describes his favourite place to collect frogspawn.

.... One day the boy hears an unfamiliar sound.

.... The boy recounts all the things he knows about frogs and frogspawn. 1 mark

Score .... /7

C These are SATs-style questions. Your answers should respond to each of the bullet points.

1 Look closely at the sentence structure in the poem.
How does the poet use sentence structure to reflect the feelings of the boy in the poem?

You should write about:

- the sentence beginning 'Here, every spring'
- the sentence beginning 'I sickened'
- the difference between the way the boy feels at the beginning of the poem and the end.

....

....

....

....

....

....

....

.... 4 marks

2 **How does the poet use sensory images to make the reader feel involved in the poem?**

You should write about:

- specific images from the poem
- how the poet appeals to the reader's senses.

....

....

....

....

....

....

....

....

....

....

....

.... 6 marks

Score .... /10

TOTAL SCORE /22

For more help on this topic see KS3 English Success Guide pages 19–25

'BLACKBERRY PICKING'

A Choose just one answer, a, b, c or d.

1 Which of the following voices can you hear in the poem?
a) the adult poet only
b) the adult poet and his mother
c) the poet as a child only
d) the adult poet and the poet as a child

2 'summer's blood was in it' is
a) a simile
b) personification
c) onomatopoeia
d) alliteration

3 Which statement best describes the way rhyme is used in this poem?
a) there is no rhyme scheme
b) the poem is written in rhyming couplets
c) the poem uses half rhyme and complete end rhymes
d) the poem has an 'abab' rhyme scheme

4 As the berries ripen they change colour. Choose the correct order:
a) grey, green, purple, red
b) green, red, purple, grey
c) red, grey, purple, green
d) purple, green, red, grey

5 What happens to the berries at the end of the poem?
a) a rat eats them
b) somebody steals them from the byre
c) the fruit ferments and turns into wine
d) they rot

Score .... /5

B Answer all parts of all questions.

1 Write down two similes used in the first stanza and explain why each is effective.

Simile: ....

Explanation: ....

....

....

Simile: ....

Explanation: ....

....

.... 4 marks

2 Find two words in the second stanza which link to 'Bluebeard' in the first stanza. Explain why the poet has used the image these words help to create.

Words used: ....

Explanation: ....

....

.... 3 marks

Score .... /7

C These are SATs-style questions. Your answers should respond to each of the bullet points.

1 The first stanza of the poem uses images connected to life and blood, e.g. 'purple clot'. **Explain why these images are used and how they can be connected to Bluebeard.**

You should write about:

- specific vocabulary and images
- the connection between life/blood, Bluebeard and what the boy is doing.

....

....

....

....

....

....

....

....

....

.... 5 marks

2 **What techniques does the poet use to show how the child's emotions change from the first stanza to the second stanza of the poem?**

You should write about:

- vocabulary choices and imagery
- the way that movement is described
- sentence length and structure.

....

....

....

....

....

....

....

....

....

.... 5 marks

Score .... /10

TOTAL SCORE /22

For more help on this topic see KS3 English Success Guide pages 18–25

COMPARING TWO POEMS

A Choose just one answer, a, b, c or d.

1 In both poems which answer best describes the emotions represented?
a) fear turns to excitement
b) boredom turns to fear
c) excitement turns to disappointment and fear
d) curiosity turns to boredom

2 Which type of imagery is used most in the two poems?
a) simile
b) personification
c) metaphor
d) oxymoron

3 Which answer best describes the main voice in the two poems?
a) adult writing about adult experience
b) child writing about childhood experience
c) child writing about adult experience
d) adult writing about childhood experience

4 The theme of the two poems is
a) being frightened of nature
b) losing childhood innocence
c) eating blackberries and catching frogspawn
d) wishing to be young again

5 What is the main difference in the structure of the two poems?
a) the number of stanzas
b) sentence length
c) use of enjambment
d) rhyme

Score .... /5

B Answer all parts of all questions.

1 In both poems the poet uses a mixture of long and short sentences to represent different emotions.
Write down the emotion(s) that each sentence type represents.

Long sentences: ....

Short sentences: .... 2 marks

2 In both poems the poet uses images or vocabulary to describe childhood experience that a child wouldn't use. **Give an example from each poem and explain what it adds to the poem.**

Example: ....

Explanation: ....

Example: ....

Explanation: .... 4 marks

3 **Write down three similarities between the two poems.**

1 ....

2 ....

3 .... 1 mark

Score .... /7

C This is a SATs-style question. Your answer should respond to each of the bullet points.

1 **Compare the ways in which the poet recreates his memories of childhood in the poems 'Death of a Naturalist' and 'Blackberry Picking'.**

You should write about:

- the way the setting and actions are described
- the emotions he felt
- the structure, imagery and vocabulary used in the poems.

....

....

....

....

....

....

....

....

....

....

....

....

....

....

....

....

....

....

....

....

....

....

.... 10 marks

Score .... /10

TOTAL SCORE /22

For more help on this topic see KS3 English Success Guide pages 18–25

AUTOBIOGRAPHY/RECOUNT

This extract is from Nelson Mandela's autobiography *Long Walk to Freedom*. He writes about his rural African upbringing; his struggle against apartheid; his imprisonment and finally his election as President of South Africa. This extract is from the section entitled 'Robben Island: The Dark Years' in which he describes his prison life.

Read the extract and answer the questions that follow.

In the midst of breakfast, the guards would yell, 'Val in! Val in!' (Fall in! Fall in!), and we would stand outside our cells for inspection. Each prisoner was required to have the three buttons of his khaki jacket properly buttoned. We were required to doff our hats as the warder walked by. If our buttons were undone, our hats unremoved, or our cells untidy, we were charged with a violation of the prison code and punished with either solitary confinement or the loss of meals.

After inspection we would work in the courtyard hammering stones until noon. There were no breaks; if we slowed down the warders would yell at us to speed up. At noon, the bell would clang for lunch and another metal drum of food would be wheeled into the courtyard. For Africans, lunch consisted of boiled mealies, that is, coarse kernels of corn. The Indians and Coloured prisoners received samp, or mealie rice, which consisted of ground mealies in a soup-like mixture. The samp was sometimes served with vegetables, whereas our mealies were served straight.

For lunch we often received phuzamandla, which means 'drink of strength', a powder made from mealies and a bit of yeast. It is meant to be stirred into water or milk, and when it is thick it can be tasty, but the prison authorities gave us so little of the powder that it barely coloured the water. I would usually save my powder for several days until I had enough to make a proper drink, but if the authorities discovered you were hoarding food, the powder was confiscated and you were punished.

After lunch we worked until 4, when the guards blew shrill whistles and we once again lined up to be counted and inspected. We were then permitted half an hour to clean up. The bathroom at the end of our corridor had two seawater showers, a saltwater tap and three large galvanized metal buckets, which were used as bathtubs. There was no hot water. We would stand or squat in these buckets, soaping ourselves with the brackish water, rinsing off the dust from the day. To wash yourself with cold water when it is cold outside is not pleasant, but we made the best of it. We would sometimes sing while washing, which made the water seem less icy. In those early days, this was one of the only times when we could converse.

Precisely at 4.30 there would be a loud knock on the wooden door at the end of the corridor, which meant that supper had been delivered. Common-law prisoners used to dish out the food to us and we would return to our cells to eat it. We again received mealie pap porridge, sometimes with the odd carrot or piece of cabbage or beetroot thrown in — but one usually had to search for it. If we did get a vegetable, we would usually have the same one for weeks on end, until the cabbage or carrots were old and mouldy and we thoroughly sick of them. Every other day we received a small piece of meat with our porridge. The meat was mostly gristle.

For supper, Coloured and Indian prisoners received a quarter loaf of bread (known as katkopf that is, a cat's head, after the shape of the bread) and a slab of margarine. Africans, it was presumed, did not care for bread as it was a 'European' type of food.

Typically, we received even less than the scanty amounts stipulated in the regulations. This was because the kitchen was rife with smuggling. The cooks — all of whom were common-law prisoners — kept the best food for themselves or their friends. Often they would lay aside the tastiest morsel for the warders in exchange for favours or preferential treatment.

At 8 p.m. the night warder would lock himself in the corridor with us, passing the key through a small hole in the door to another warder outside. The warder would then walk up and down the corridor, ordering us to go to sleep. No cry of 'lights out' was ever given on Robben Island because the single mesh-covered bulb in our cell burned day and night. Later, those studying for higher degrees were permitted to read until 10 or 11 p.m.

From *Long Walk to Freedom*
by Nelson Mandela

A Choose just one answer, a, b, c or d.

1 *Katkopf* means
a) drink of strength
b) fall in
c) lights out
d) cat's head

2 Prisoners had to go to sleep at
a) 7 p.m.
b) 8 p.m.
c) 10 p.m.
d) 11 p.m.

3 Which of the following is not a feature of a recount text?
a) written in the present tense
b) temporal (time) connectives
c) events told in order
d) focuses on specified individuals or groups

4 When was inspection?
a) before breakfast
b) after breakfast
c) during breakfast
d) before lights out

5 Africans didn't receive bread because
a) they didn't like it
b) the common-law prisoners stole it
c) the prison authorities thought they didn't like 'European food'
d) it was kept back as punishment

Score .... /5

B Answer all parts of all questions.

1 Which part of the prison routine is described in most detail? Explain what this detail emphasises. Find and copy a quotation to support your explanation.

Part of routine: ....

Explanation: ....

....

Quotation: .... 3 marks

2 This is a recount text. Find and copy an example of each of the following features of a recount.

Temporal connective: ....

Focuses on individuals or identified groups: ....

.... 2 marks

3 This extract uses language from another country. Find an example and explain how the meaning has been made clear to the reader.

Example: ....

Explanation: ....

.... 2 marks

Score .... /7

C

This is a SATs-style question. Your answer should respond to each of the bullet points.

1 **Explain how the writer highlights the harshness of the routine and the prejudice he encountered whilst in prison.**

You should write about:

- the way he describes the daily routine
- what he does to cope with the routine
- his relationships with others
- punishments.

....

....

....

....

....

....

....

....

....

....

....

....

....

....

....

....

....

....

....

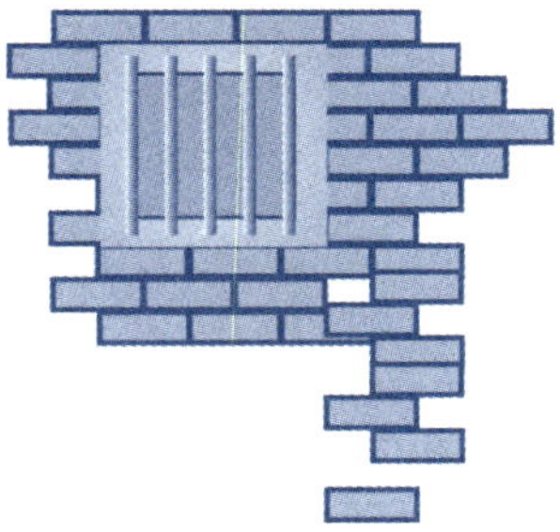

....

....

....

....10 marks

Score .... /10

TOTAL SCORE /22

For more help on this topic see KS3 English Success Guide pages 26–33

Digitising & Restoring
Tapes & Records on Your PC

A PC with a CD burner and soundcard provides the ideal means to preserve old tape recordings or transfer your vinyl collection to CD

Martin Walker

One of the reasons many PC users have for buying a soundcard is to transfer recordings from older analogue media such as vinyl or tape, and burn them to CD so that they can easily be listened to and archived. In this month's PC Musician I'm going to take you through the three stages of this process: getting the audio from your tape or record into the PC, carrying out any processing or restoration work that may be appropriate, and burning it to CD.

Preparing Your Material

The obvious thing to ensure first of all is that whatever analogue playback device you're using to get the audio into your computer, be it a reel-to-reel or cassette tape deck or a turntable, is set up to yield the best possible audio quality. If you're using a tape machine, for instance, make sure that the heads and mechanism are cleaned, and it's also worth cleaning vinyl records properly before you transfer them.

The output of tape decks can be directly connected to a suitable line-level input on your soundcard. Most cassette decks will have -10dBV consumer output levels, while more professional reel-to-reel tape machines will need your soundcard's +4dBU input sensitivity setting. If you're transferring records, however, you'll need to amplify and correctly equalise the low output level from your record deck's magnetic cartridge before you can connect it to a soundcard. Typical signal levels are around 5mV from an MM (moving magnet) pick up, and 0.5mV from an MC (moving coil) pickup, so you should keep the deck well away from both your PC and its CRT monitor.

Many musicians will still have hi-fis with a suitable phono input, and some mixers provide them, but otherwise you'll need a preamp with the RIAA (Recording Industries Association of America) equalisation that provides a flat overall frequency response. Phono preamps are available as stand-alone boxes from various specialist hi-fi retailers, and in DIY form from companies like Maplin (www.maplin.co.uk) but soundcard manufacturers have also spotted this niche. Terratec, for instance, offer a stand-alone phono preamp that draws its power from the 15-pin Gameport connector found on many consumer soundcards, while you can buy Steinberg's low-cost *Clean!* software (reviewed in *SOS* July 1999) bundled with an RIAA preamp for £79.99. Most phono preamps will probably have the lower -10dBV output level.

Here's a carefully tweaked RIAA de-emphasis curve that's provided by Waves in their collection of Q10 pre/De-Emphasis presets. Notice the 12dB on the input faders to prevent digital overload.

If you don't have a dedicated RIAA-compatible preamp, you could try using a mic preamp and then an EQ plug-in to boost the bass end and roll off the treble

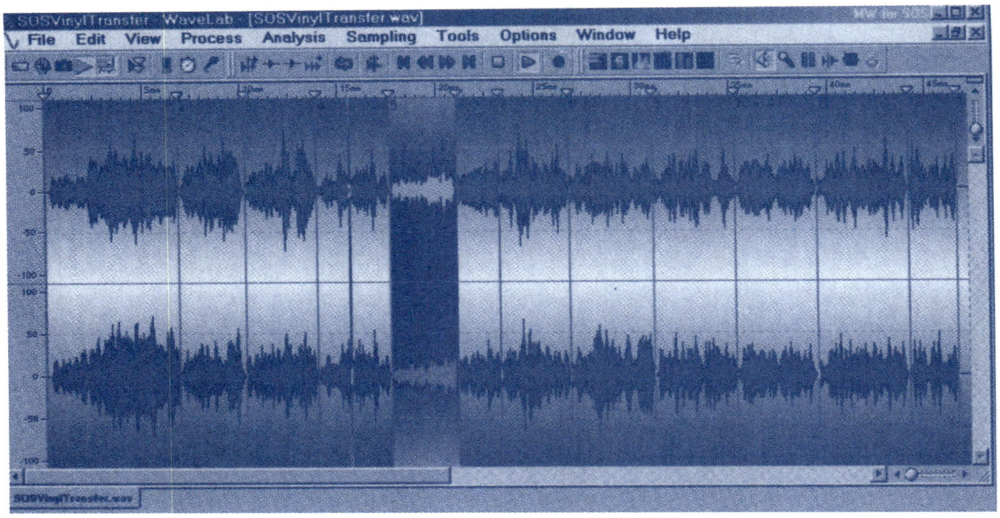

With a suitable editor like *Wavelab*, you can keep an entire album's worth of tracks in one file using suitable markers, and process them on a global or individual basis.

end to compensate for the response of the cutting lathe. I've detailed some suitable settings in the RIAA Equalisation Using An EQ Plug-in box.

When it comes to actually playing back your tapes, it's important to get the right playback settings on your tape recorder. Obviously, you should set up cassette recorders appropriately for ferrochrome, chrome or metal tapes, while reel-to-reel recorders may give you a choice between IEC or NAB playback EQ (although this can be corrected once in the PC using a suitable EQ plug-in such as Waves' *Q10*). For most recordings, you'll also need to decide whether or not you need noise reduction enabled, and if so of which type—Dolby A, B or C, Dbx and so on. Nearly all prerecorded cassettes use Dolby B, but if you don't know what type was used on a particular recording, it's often possible to guess. If you hear background noise levels 'pumping' with noise reduction switched out, the chances are that the recording used noise reduction, and most likely Dolby B. If you don't know, choose the type that gives the most natural-sounding result compared with other known recordings.

Recording Into A Soundcard

I can see little point in using a soundcard sample rate other than 44.1kHz if you're transferring audio to be put on CD, while 16-bit recording should provide more than enough dynamic range to capture any analogue tape. However, vinyl freaks with pristine record collections may want to instead choose 88.2kHz and 24-bit, to preserve the maximum amount of detail and high-frequency extension until the last possible moment. If you've got a consumer soundcard with loads of inputs like the Soundblaster Live! range, make sure you mute all but the one you're using, to minimise background noise levels.

It's best to experiment a little to find the optimum recording level, to make sure you get the maximum dynamic range onto the hard disk recording. Many PC audio recording applications and soundcard utilities provide an input meter with text readout of the highest recorded level, so start by running through a couple of tracks to see what this is, and then adjust the output level of your tape player or mixer accordingly, so that you still have one or two dBs of headroom left. For instance, if your peak meter reads -5dB, you can safely increase input level by at least 3dB without worrying about running into clipping. If you know the recordings well, you'll probably already know where the loudest parts are likely to be. You may well only have to do this once for a particular deck, and can then run through a whole batch of tapes or records with the same settings, so it's worth doing carefully.

Before you get stuck in, take a careful look at the recording facilities offered by your audio application, since there may be some real time-savers among them. For instance, *Wavelab* provides a selection of auto-start and auto-stop options that can automate the process of recording albums. I find its 'Auto-create markers at silence points' function particularly useful, since it places suitable CD track markers in gaps in the audio. Although you'll probably have to move their positions forward so that they coincide with the start of the next track rather than the fade out of the previous one, it's better than doing everything by hand.

Before you hit Record, check that you've got enough hard drive space. At 10Mb per stereo minute at 44.1 kHz/16-bit, you'll need about 650Mb per CD, and if you envisage doing any PC audio editing you'll need double this amount of space to store the temporary files. During vinyl transfers you should keep your monitor levels quiet: otherwise, acoustic feedback could modify the frequency response of the recording. For the same reason, avoid moving about during the recording if your floor isn't solid.

Sound on Sound
August 2002

A Choose just one answer, a, b, c or d.

1 This article explains how to
- a) make your own original recordings
- b) transfer tape and vinyl recordings to CD
- c) make music using your PC
- d) listen to music via the internet

2 MM stands for
- a) moving microphone
- b) moving magnet
- c) micro-magnet
- d) music magnet

3 Audio means
- a) music
- b) speech
- c) sound
- d) recording

4 Most pre-recorded cassettes use
- a) Dolby A
- b) Dolby B
- c) Dolby C
- d) Dolby D

5 How much hard drive space do you need to record a CD on your PC?
- a) 10Mb
- b) 1300Mb
- c) 44.1kHz
- d) 650Mb

Score .... /5

B Answer all parts of all questions.

1 Give two ways you can tell this article is aimed at a specialist audience.

....

.... 2 marks

2 This article sets out to explain a three-stage process. In your own words, briefly explain what the three stages are.

1) ....

2) ....

3) .... 3 marks

3 This article uses logical and temporal (sequence) connectives. Find and copy an example of each.

Logical connective: ....

Temporal connective: .... 1 mark

4 Look at the paragraph beginning 'If you don't have a dedicated...'. Find and copy the (modal auxiliary) verb which indicates that advice is being given.

....

.... 1 mark

Score .... /7

C This is a SATs-style question. Your answer should respond to each of the bullet points.

1 **Comment on the effectiveness of the language and layout in this article.**

You should write about:

- the intended purpose and audience of the article
- use of technical language, formal and informal language
- the use of pictures, headings and subheadings
- overall organisation.

....

.... 10 marks

Score .... /10

TOTAL SCORE /22

For more help on this topic see KS3 English Success Guide pages 26–27

PERSUASION AND ARGUMENT

Read the two extracts and answer the questions that follow.

The extract printed below is the final part of a speech delivered by the Reverend Martin Luther King at a civil rights march in Washington (28 August 1963).

I have a dream ...

So I say to you, my friends, that even though we must face the difficulties of today and tomorrow, I still have a dream. It is a dream deeply rooted in the American dream that one day this nation will rise up and live out the true meaning of its creed — we hold these truths to be self-evident, that all men are created equal.

I have a dream that one day on the red hills of Georgia, sons of former slaves and sons of former slave-owners will be able to sit down together at the table of brotherhood.

I have a dream that one day, even the state of Mississippi, a state sweltering with the heat of injustice, sweltering with the heat of oppression, will be transformed into an oasis of freedom and justice.

I have a dream that my four little children will one day live in a nation where they will not be judged by the colour of their skin but by the content of their character. I have a dream today!

I have a dream that one day, down in Alabama, with its vicious racists, with its governor having his lips dripping with the words of interposition and nullification, that one day, right there in Alabama, little black boys and black girls will be able to join hands with little white boys and white girls as sisters and brothers. I have a dream today!

I have a dream that one day every valley shall be exalted, every hill and mountain shall be made low, the rough places shall be made plain, and the crooked places shall be made straight and the glory of the Lord will be revealed and all flesh shall see it together.

This is our hope. This is the faith that I go back to the South with.

With this faith we will be able to bear out of the mountain of despair a stone of hope. With this faith we will be able to transform the jangling discord of our nation into a beautiful symphony of brotherhood.

With this faith we will be able to work together, to pray together, to struggle together, to go to jail together, to stand up for freedom together; knowing that we will be free one day. This will be the day when all of God's children will be able to sing with new meaning — 'my country 'tis of thee; sweet land of liberty, land where my fathers died, land of the pilgrim's pride; from every mountain side, let freedom ring' — and if America is to be a great nation, this must become true.

So let freedom ring from the prodigious hilltops of New Hampshire.

Let freedom ring from the mighty mountains of New York.

Let freedom ring from the heightening Alleghenies of Pennsylvania.

Let freedom ring from the snow-capped Rockies of Colorado.

Let freedom ring from the curvaceous slopes of California.

But not only that.

Let freedom ring from Stone Mountain of Georgia.

Let freedom ring from Lookout Mountain of Tennessee.

Let freedom ring from every hill and molehill of Mississippi, from every mountain side, let freedom ring.

When we let freedom ring, when we let it ring from every village and every hamlet, from every state and every city, we will be able to speed up that day when all of God's children, black men and white men, Jews and Gentiles, Protestants and Catholics, will be able to join hands and sing in the words of the old Negro spiritual, 'Free at last! free at last! thank God Almighty, we are free at last!'

The writer of the following passage argues that watching television can be bad for your health.

Too much television can damage your child's health

Television may be part of everyday life for most children but is it safe? In our hectic lives we are so busy managing our private and professional concerns and relationships, we allow our children to spend a huge percentage of their unsupervised time watching television. So busy, in fact, that most of us don't stop to consider the hidden dangers of unlimited viewing.

The health risks which attend excessive television viewing are extensive and, to my mind, should not be underestimated. It contributes to the growing problems of adolescent obesity; it prevents regular exercise which could cause heart problems in later life; it causes psychological problems if children are exposed to inappropriate materials and it can damage eyesight.

However, the most worrying problem is the detrimental effect that too much television can have on the early stages of a child's development. Playing games, listening to stories and interacting with other children are all essential to a child's emotional, physical and communicational development. When television takes the place of these activities, we allow untold damage to be done.

Of course, many would be quick to defend the educational value of television and there is no doubt that properly managed television viewing can be beneficial. In my opinion, however, the dangers far outweigh the benefits. Until parents make time to exercise proper control over their children's viewing habits, children's health will continue to suffer.

A Choose just one answer, a, b, c or d.

1 **The persuasive technique used most in Martin Luther King's speech is**
a) rhetorical question
b) emotive language
c) repetition
d) short exclamatory sentences

2 **Which of the following pronouns are used most in the speech?**
a) he and she
b) I and we
c) you and it
d) us and them

3 **The intended audience of *Too much television* is**
a) health professionals
b) teachers
c) children
d) adults – particularly parents

4 **The sentence type used most in *Too much television* is**
a) simple
b) complex
c) compound
d) interrogative

5 **The title *Too much television can damage your child's health* is**
a) a fact
b) an opinion
c) an opinion presented as fact
d) a fact presented as opinion

Score .... /5

B Answer all parts of all questions.

These questions all relate to 'Too much television can damage your child's health'.

1 Find and copy two connective words or phrases used in the passage.

1) ....

2) .... 1 mark

2 What type of question is used in the first sentence? Explain the effect of opening the text in this way.

Question type: ....

Explanation: ....

.... 2 marks

3 Give two examples of problems caused by too much television viewing and explain why these problems occur.

Example: ....

Explanation: ....

....

Example: ....

Explanation: ....

.... 4 marks

Score .... /7

C

This is a SATs-style question. Your answer should respond to each of the bullet points.

These questions all relate to 'I have a dream'.

1 **Give two examples of words, phrases or themes that are repeated in the speech and explain how each is used to add emphasis.**

Example: ....

Explanation: ....

Example: ....

Explanation: .... 4 marks

2 **How does the writer use sentence structure to control the pace and emphasis of the speech?**

You should write about:

- sentence length
- use of repetitive structures
- the final sentences in paragraphs 4 and 5
- the penultimate sentence.

....

....

....

....

....

....

....

....

....

....

....

....

....

....

.... 6 marks

Score .... /10

TOTAL SCORE /22

For more help on this topic see KS3 English Success Guide pages 26–29

MEDIA TEXT

This leaflet was produced by a large supermarket chain to encourage healthy eating. It gives information about the benefits of healthy eating and recommendations about daily intake of fruit and vegetables. It also aims to persuade shoppers to buy produce from their supermarket chain.

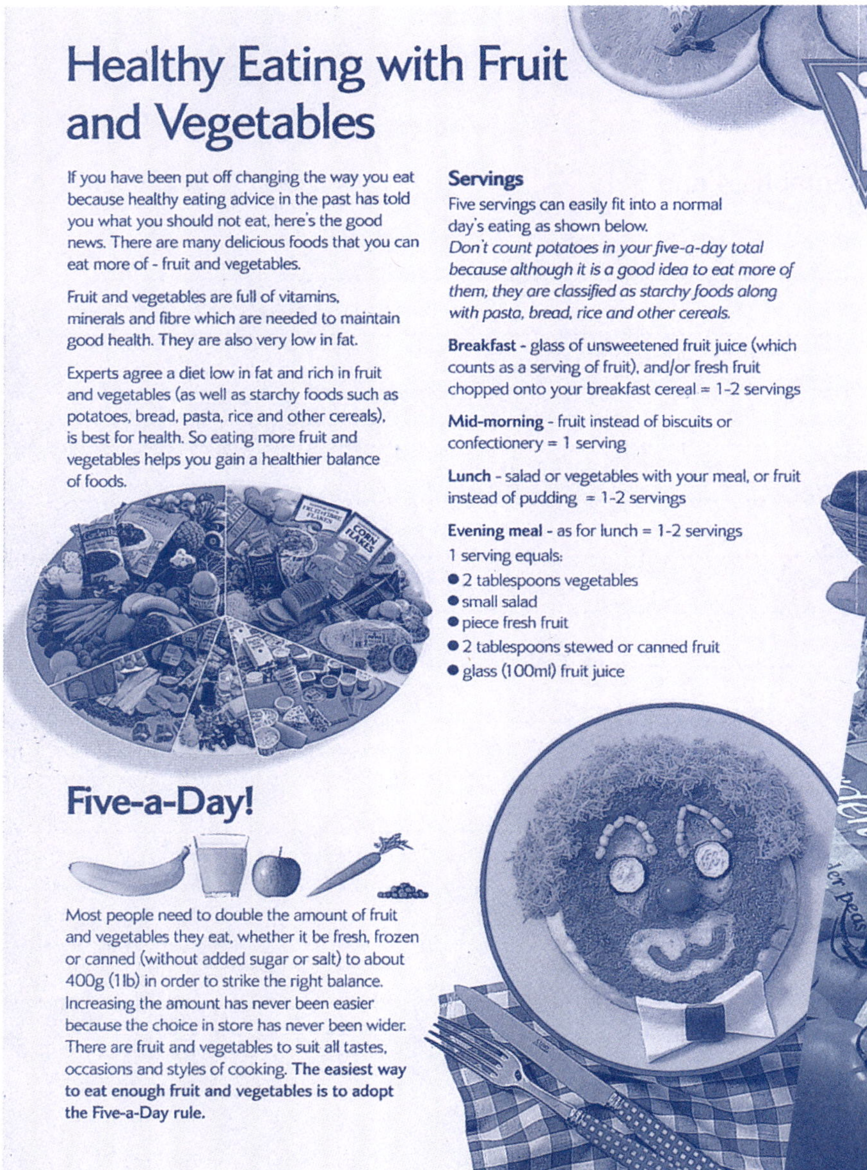

Healthy Eating with Fruit and Vegetables

If you have been put off changing the way you eat because healthy eating advice in the past has told you what you should not eat, here's the good news. There are many delicious foods that you can eat more of - fruit and vegetables.

Fruit and vegetables are full of vitamins, minerals and fibre which are needed to maintain good health. They are also very low in fat.

Experts agree a diet low in fat and rich in fruit and vegetables (as well as starchy foods such as potatoes, bread, pasta, rice and other cereals), is best for health. So eating more fruit and vegetables helps you gain a healthier balance of foods.

Servings

Five servings can easily fit into a normal day's eating as shown below.

Don't count potatoes in your five-a-day total because although it is a good idea to eat more of them, they are classified as starchy foods along with pasta, bread, rice and other cereals.

Breakfast - glass of unsweetened fruit juice (which counts as a serving of fruit), and/or fresh fruit chopped onto your breakfast cereal = 1-2 servings

Mid-morning - fruit instead of biscuits or confectionery = 1 serving

Lunch - salad or vegetables with your meal, or fruit instead of pudding = 1-2 servings

Evening meal - as for lunch = 1-2 servings

1 serving equals:

- 2 tablespoons vegetables
- small salad
- piece fresh fruit
- 2 tablespoons stewed or canned fruit
- glass (100ml) fruit juice

Five-a-Day!

Most people need to double the amount of fruit and vegetables they eat, whether it be fresh, frozen or canned (without added sugar or salt) to about 400g (1lb) in order to strike the right balance. Increasing the amount has never been easier because the choice in store has never been wider. There are fruit and vegetables to suit all tastes, occasions and styles of cooking. **The easiest way to eat enough fruit and vegetables is to adopt the Five-a-Day rule.**

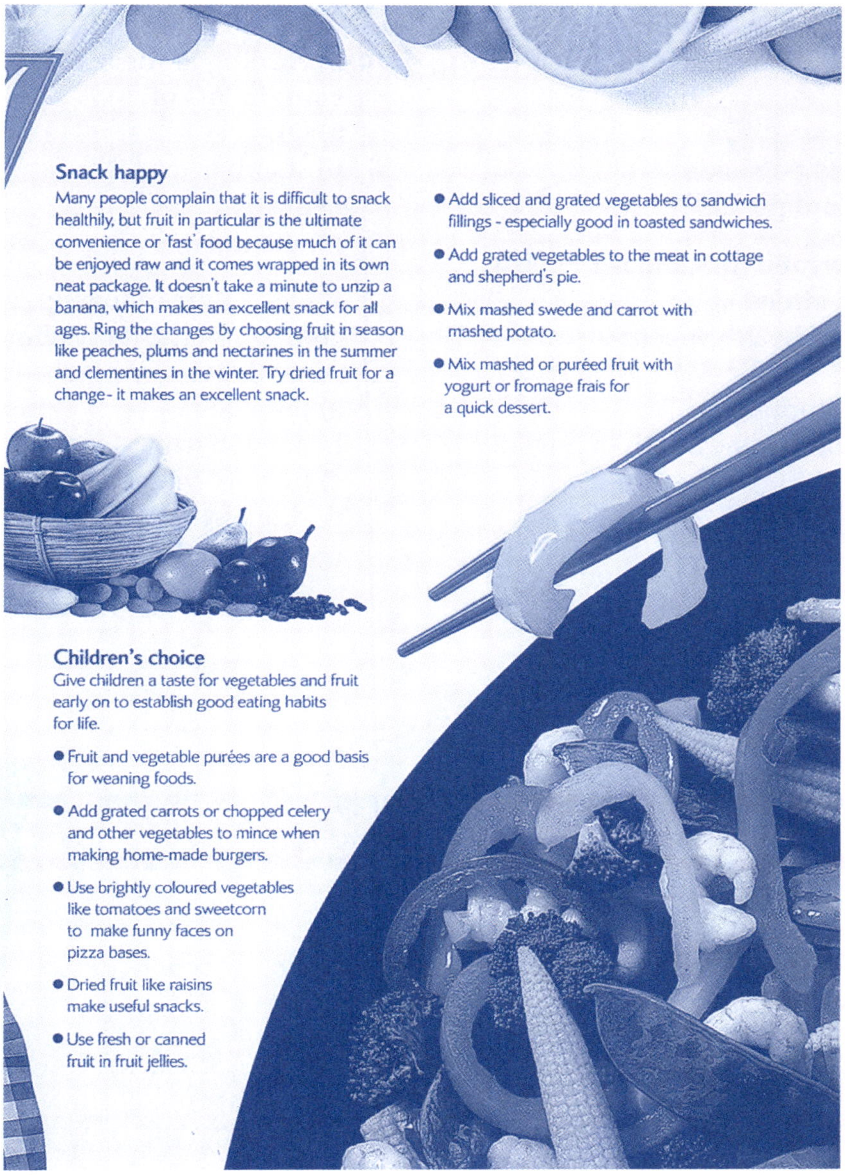

Snack happy

Many people complain that it is difficult to snack healthily, but fruit in particular is the ultimate convenience or 'fast' food because much of it can be enjoyed raw and it comes wrapped in its own neat package. It doesn't take a minute to unzip a banana, which makes an excellent snack for all ages. Ring the changes by choosing fruit in season like peaches, plums and nectarines in the summer and clementines in the winter. Try dried fruit for a change- it makes an excellent snack.

- Add sliced and grated vegetables to sandwich fillings - especially good in toasted sandwiches.
- Add grated vegetables to the meat in cottage and shepherd's pie.
- Mix mashed swede and carrot with mashed potato.
- Mix mashed or puréed fruit with yogurt or fromage frais for a quick dessert.

Children's choice

Give children a taste for vegetables and fruit early on to establish good eating habits for life.

- Fruit and vegetable purées are a good basis for weaning foods.
- Add grated carrots or chopped celery and other vegetables to mince when making home-made burgers.
- Use brightly coloured vegetables like tomatoes and sweetcorn to make funny faces on pizza bases.
- Dried fruit like raisins make useful snacks.
- Use fresh or canned fruit in fruit jellies.

A Choose just one answer, a, b, c or d.

1 The purpose of this text is to
a) entertain
b) describe
c) explain and persuade
d) describe and persuade

2 The text is written in Standard English because it is aimed at
a) doctors and health specialists
b) children
c) ordinary shoppers
d) people living in the South of England

3 This leaflet contains
a) facts only
b) a mixture of fact and opinion
c) opinions only
d) instructions only

4 According to the leaflet fruit and vegetables contain lots of
a) fat
b) starch
c) protein
d) vitamins

5 Which of the following shouldn't be counted in the daily allowance of fruit and vegetables?
a) potatoes
b) canned fruit
c) frozen vegetables
d) dried fruit

Score .... **/5**

B Answer all parts of all questions.

1 Which verb form is used in the 'Children's Choice' section of the leaflet? Explain why this form is used.

Verb form: ....

Explanation: .... 2 marks

2 Identify two layout/presentation features in the leaflet and explain why they have been used.

Layout: ....

Explanation: ....

Layout: ....

Explanation: .... 2 marks

3 'Take 5!' is a common expression. Explain why it is an appropriate title for this text.

....

....

....

.... 3 marks

Score .... **/7**

C This is a SATs-style question. Your answer should respond to each of the bullet points.

1 **How does the leaflet aim to persuade people to buy and eat more fruit and vegetables?**

You should write about:

- the language used
- the layout of the leaflet
- whether you think the leaflet will be successful.

10 marks

Score .... **/10**

TOTAL SCORE /22

For more help on this topic see KS3 English Success Guide pages 36–43

WRITING TO DESCRIBE

A

Choose just one answer, a, b, c or d / true or false.

1 **Descriptive writing is**
a) always factual
b) always fiction
c) always a balance of fact and fiction
d) can be a mixture of fact and fiction

2 **An adverb**
a) describes a noun
b) usually ends in –ed
c) describes a verb
d) is a doing word

3 **When you are describing a person you should concentrate on what they look like.**
true/false

4 **Imagery such as simile and metaphor can be used in description.**
true/false

5 **Sensory description is writing that**
a) describes your senses
b) describes what you can see
c) describes what you can hear
d) describes what you can see, hear, touch, taste or smell

Score .... **/5**

B

Although this section doesn't carry a score, it will help you to score higher marks in Section C.

Use the space below to complete a spider diagram plan for the writing task in Section C.

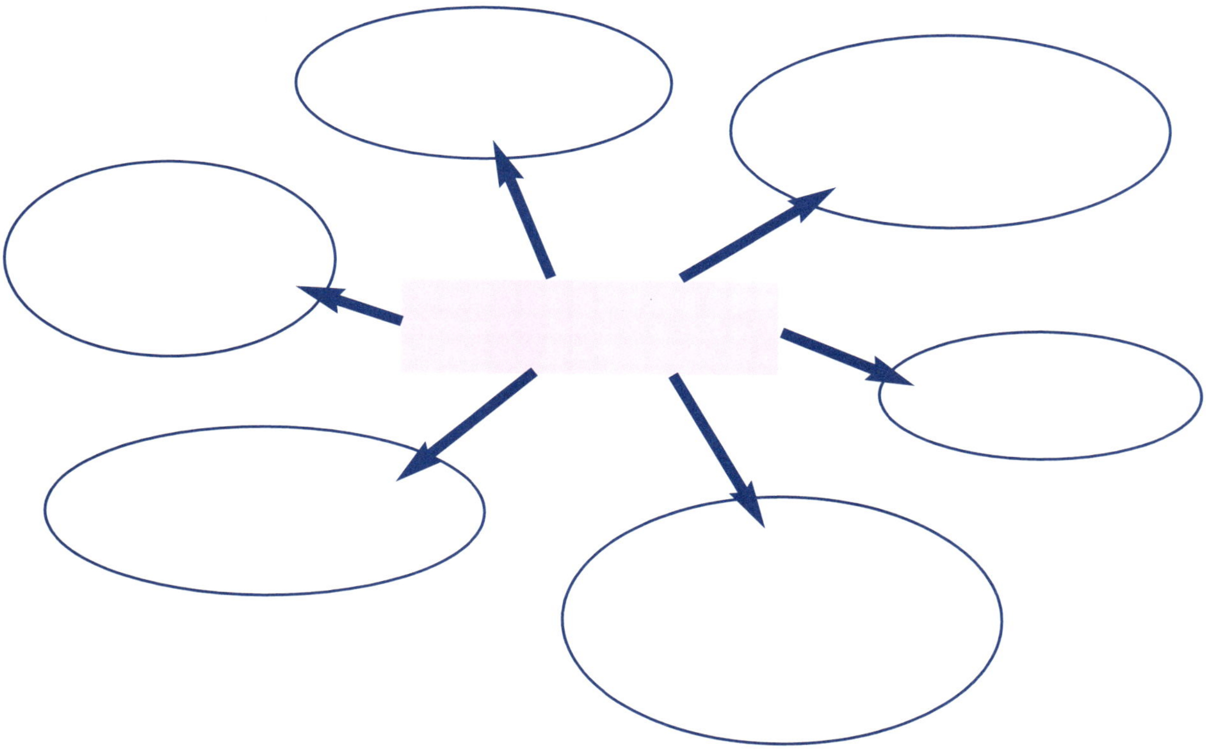

C

This is a SATs-style question. Your answer should respond to each of the bullet points. You should spend about 20 minutes writing. Continue your writing on a separate sheet if necessary.

1 **Write a brief description of your ideal holiday location. Write three paragraphs only.**

You could describe:

- the setting
- the atmosphere
- the people.

Remember to use descriptive vocabulary and imagery; try to appeal to the senses.

....

....

....

....

....

....

....

....

....

....

....

....

....

....

....

....

....

....

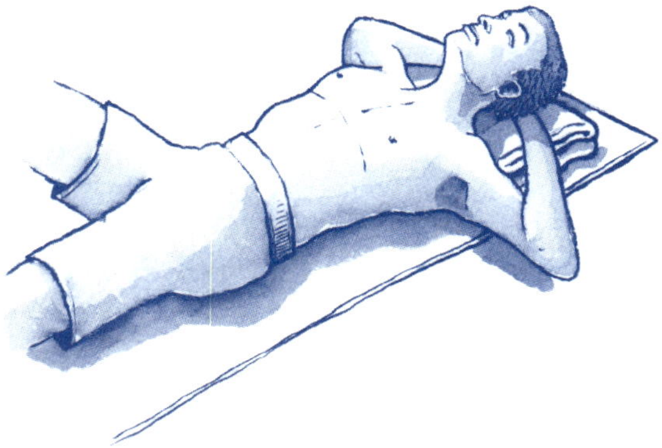

....

....

....

....

.... 20 marks

Score .... /20

TOTAL SCORE /25

For more help on this topic see KS3 English Success Guide pages 47–49

WRITING TO IMAGINE, EXPLORE, ENTERTAIN

A

Choose just one answer, a, b, c or d / true or false.

1 **The structure of narrative writing is usually**
a) introduction, development, resolution, climax
b) resolution, climax, introduction, development
c) introduction, development, climax, resolution
d) introduction, climax, development, resolution

2 **The most important element(s) of narrative fiction is/are**
a) plot, description and dialogue
b) plot
c) dialogue
d) plot and dialogue

3 **An adjective**
a) usually ends in –ly
b) describes a noun
c) describes a verb
d) usually ends in –ed

4 **You should reveal everything about a character directly.**
true/false

5 **Dialogue should always be followed by a phrase such as 'Jamie said' to indicate who has spoken.**
true/false

Score .... /5

B

Although this section doesn't carry a score, it will help you to score higher marks in Section C.

Use the space below to complete a plan for the writing task in Section C.

Main character factfile

....

....

....

....

....

....

....

....

....

....

....

Introduction

....

....

Development

....

....

Climax

....

....

Resolution

....

....

C

This is a SATs-style question. The bullet points are suggestions to help you complete the task. You should spend about 40 minutes writing. You should continue your writing on a separate sheet. Try not to write more than two sides of A4 paper.

Several of the Reading Fiction examples in this book have been about frightening experiences.

1 Imagine that you are trapped somewhere. Write the story of your escape.

You could:

- describe the place where you are trapped
- describe your feelings
- build up a tense or frightening atmosphere
- if you prefer to write in the third person you could write about somebody else being trapped.

Remember to include a balance of plot development, description and dialogue.

....

30 marks

Score .... /30

TOTAL SCORE /35

For more help on this topic see KS3 English Success Guide pages 46–55

WRITING TO ARGUE AND PERSUADE

A Choose just one answer, a, b, c or d / true or false.

1 Opinions would not be used in persuasive writing.
true/false

2 A counter argument is
a) a point which supports the main argument
b) a point which opposes the main argument
c) an argument that offends somebody
d) an irrelevant point

3 Which of the following could be used as a rhetorical question?
a) What is your name?
b) What do you mean?
c) If you feel the same way why don't you join us?
d) What is your favourite colour?

4 If you begin a formal letter *Dear Sir* you should end with
a) Yours sincerely
b) Yours faithfully
c) Best wishes
d) yours sincerely

5 When hand writing a letter your own address should be written
a) at the top right
b) at the bottom right
c) at the top left
d) under the recipient's address

Score .... /5

B Although this section doesn't carry a score, it will help you to score higher marks in Section C.

Use the space below to complete a plan for the writing task in Section C.

Points in favour of my argument

Use this space to record and organise the main points of your argument.

....

....

....

....

Word/phrase bank

Use this space to note down emotive words/phrases, rhetorical questions, etc.

....

....

....

....

C

This is a SATs-style question. The bullet points are suggestions to help you complete the task. You should spend about 40 minutes writing. You should continue your writing on a separate sheet. Try not to write more than two sides of A4 paper.

1 **Write a letter to your local MP to persuade him/her to support your argument that more major sporting events should take place in the UK.**

You could write about:

- the benefits for British sportsmen and sportswomen
- the benefits for local communities
- the international profile of the UK
- possible objections and how you would counter them.

Remember to write a formal letter. Try to be as persuasive as you can.

.... 30 marks

Score .... /30

TOTAL SCORE /35

For more help on this topic see KS3 English Success Guide pages 56–62

WRITING TO INFORM AND EXPLAIN

A

Choose just one answer, a, b, c or d / true or false.

1 **Information texts are usually written in the first person.**
true/false

2 **Information and explanation texts are usually written in the present tense.**
true/false

3 **Explanation texts use logical connectives. Which of the following is not a logical connective?**
a) because
b) as a result of
c) however
d) firstly

4 **Which of the following sentence types do information texts use?**
a) mostly complex
b) mostly simple
c) simple and compound
d) compound and complex

5 **Explanation texts sometimes use the passive voice. Which of the following doesn't use the passive voice?**
a) The window was broken.
b) John broke the window.
c) The window was broken by John.
d) The window was broken accidentally.

Score .... /5

B

Although this section doesn't carry a score, it will help you to score higher marks in Section C.

Use the space below to complete a plan for the writing task in Section C.
Use this space to brainstorm information about teenage fashion.

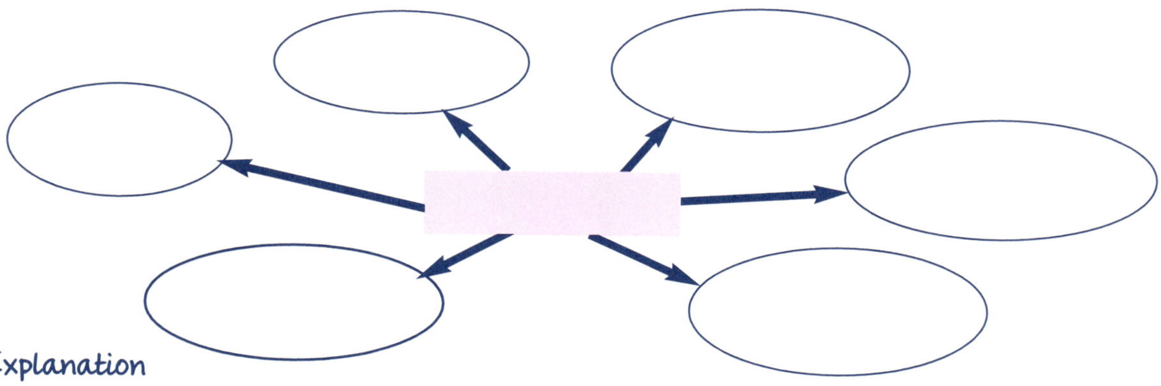

Explanation
Make brief notes to explain why different people choose different styles.

....

....

....

....

....

C

This is a SATs-style question. Your answer should respond to each of the bullet points. You should spend about 20 minutes writing. Continue your writing on a separate sheet if necessary.

Fashions change very quickly and different groups of people like to wear different styles of clothing.

1 **Write three paragraphs to inform the reader about current teenage fashion and explain why different people choose to follow different fashions.**

You could write about:

- clothes and hairstyles
- the influence of music and celebrities on fashion.

Remember to write in the third person and present tense.

....

....

....

....

....

....

....

....

....

....

....

....

....

....

....

....

....

....

....

....

....

.... 20 marks

Score .... /20

TOTAL SCORE /25

For more help on this topic see KS3 English Success Guide pages 56–57

WRITING TO REVIEW, ANALYSE, COMMENT

A Choose just one answer, a, b, c or d / true or false.

1 A review should contain
- a) fact only
- b) fact and opinion
- c) opinion only
- d) opinions presented as fact

2 A review should explore the strengths and weaknesses of the piece being reviewed.
true/false

3 Comment and analysis texts should contain
- a) statements and explanations
- b) statements and explanations supported by textual evidence
- c) long quotations without explanation
- d) unsupported opinions

4 Analysis texts should be written in
- a) first person
- b) second person
- c) first and third person
- d) third person

5 Review texts can be written in the first or third person.
true/false

Score .... /5

B Although this section doesn't carry a score, it will help you to score higher marks in Section C.

Use the space below to complete a plan for the writing task in Section C.

Make brief notes under the following headings:

Strengths

....

....

....

Weaknesses

....

....

....

Recommendations

....

....

....

....

C

This is a SATs-style question. Your answer should respond to each of the bullet points. You should spend about 20 minutes writing. Continue your writing on a separate sheet if necessary.

1 **Write a brief review of a book you have read or a film you have seen recently. Write three paragraphs only.**

You could include:

- information about the book/film
- the strengths of the book/film
- the weaknesses of the book/film
- your recommendations to other readers/viewers.

.... 20 marks

Score .... /20

TOTAL SCORE /25

For more help on this topic see KS3 English Success Guide pages 62–63

TWELFTH NIGHT

Read the two extracts from the play and answer the questions that follow.

In this opening scene the Duke of Illyria, Orsino claims to be completely consumed by his love for Olivia. He complains about her vow to mourn for her dead brother for seven years but then sees some hope in the situation.

ACT I SCENE 1
Orsino's palace

Music. Enter ORSINO, Duke of Illyria, CURIO, and other Lords

ORSINO If music be the food of love, play on,
Give me excess of it, that surfeiting,
The appetite may sicken, and so die.
That strain again, it had a dying fall:
O, it came o'er my ear like the sweet sound
That breathes upon a bank of violets,
Stealing and giving odour. Enough, no more;
'Tis not so sweet now as it was before.
O spirit of love, how quick and fresh art thou,
That notwithstanding thy capacity,
Receiveth as the sea, nought enters there,
Of what validity and pitch soe'er,
But falls into abatement and low price
Even in a minute! So full of shapes is fancy,
That it alone is high fantastical.

CURIO Will you go hunt, my lord?

ORSINO What, Curio?

CURIO The hart.

ORSINO Why so I do, the noblest that I have.
O, when mine eyes did see Olivia first,
Methought she purg'd the air of pestilence;
That instant was I turn'd into a hart,
And my desires, like fell and cruel hounds,
E'er since pursue me.

Enter VALENTINE

How now? What news from her?

VALENTINE So please my lord, I might not be admitted,
But from her handmaid do return this answer:
The element itself, till seven years' heat,

Shall not behold her face at ample view;
But like a cloistress she will veiled walk,
And water once a day her chamber round
With eye-offending brine: all this to season
A brother's dead love, which she would keep fresh
And lasting, in her sad remembrance.

ORSINO O, she that hath a heart of that fine frame
To pay this debt of love but to a brother,
How will she love, when the rich golden shaft
Hath kill'd the flock of all affections else
That live in her; when liver, brain, and heart,
These sovereign thrones, are all supplied and fill'd
Her sweet perfections with one selfsame king!
Away before me to sweet beds of flowers!
Love-thoughts lie rich when canopied with bowers.
Exeunt

Glossary

surfeiting	over-filled
validity and pitch	high value
falls into abatement	becomes less valuable
fancy	love
high fantastical	very imaginative
hart	male deer
pestilence	plague
fell	fierce
element	air
cloistress	a nun
eye-offending brine	tears
rich golden shaft	Cupid's arrow of love

In this extract Olivia, believing Viola to be a male servant called Cesario, begins to reveal her true feelings to him.

ACT III SCENE 1 lines 88 – end
In Olivia's Orchard

OLIVIA Let the garden door be shut, and leave me to my hearing.
[Exeunt Sir Toby, Sir Andrew, and Maria]
Give me your hand, sir.
VIOLA My duty, madam, and most humble service.
OLIVIA What is your name?
VIOLA Cesario is your servant's name, fair princess.
OLIVIA My servant, sir? 'Twas never merry world
Since lowly feigning was call'd compliment:
Y'are servant to the Count Orsino, youth.

VIOLA And he is yours, and his must needs be yours:
Your servant's servant is your servant, madam.

OLIVIA For him, I think not on him; for his thoughts,
Would they were blanks, rather than fill'd with me.

VIOLA Madam, I come to whet your gentle thoughts
On his behalf.

OLIVIA O, by your leave, I pray you!
I bade you never speak again of him;
But would you undertake another suit,
I had rather hear you to solicit that,
Than music from the spheres.

VIOLA Dear lady—

OLIVIA Give me leave, beseech you. I did send,
After the last enchantment you did here,
A ring in chase of you. So did I abuse
Myself, my servant, and, I fear me, you.
Under your hard construction must I sit,
To force that on you in a shameful cunning
Which you knew none of yours. What might you think?
Have you not set mine honour at the stake,
And baited it with all th'unmuzzled thoughts
That tyrannous heart can think? To one of your receiving
Enough is shown; a cypress, not a bosom,
Hides my heart. So, let me hear you speak.

VIOLA I pity you.

OLIVIA That's a degree to love.

VIOLA No, not a grize: for 'tis a vulgar proof
That very oft we pity enemies.

OLIVIA Why then, methinks 'tis time to smile again.
O world, how apt the poor are to be proud!
If one should be a prey, how much the better
To fall before the lion than the wolf!
(Clock strikes)
The clock upbraids me with the waste of time.
Be not afraid, good youth, I will not have you.
And yet when wit and youth is come to harvest
Your wife is like to reap a proper man.
There lies your way, due west.

VIOLA Then westward ho!
Grace and good disposition attend your ladyship
You'll nothing, madam, to my lord by me?

OLIVIA Stay!
I prithee, tell me what thou think'st of me.

VIOLA That you do think you are not what you are.

OLIVIA If I think so, I think the same of you.

VIOLA Then think you right: I am not what I am.

OLIVIA I would you were as I would have you be.
VIOLA Would it be better, madam, than I am?
I wish it might, for now I am your fool.

OLIVIA *[Aside]* O what a deal of scorn looks beautiful
In the contempt and anger of his lip!
A murd'rous guilt shows not itself more soon,
Than love that would seem hid. Love's night is noon.
Cesario, by the roses of the spring,
By maidhood, honour, truth, and everything,
I love thee so that, maugre all thy pride,
Nor wit nor reason can my passion hide.
Do not extort thy reasons from this clause.
For that I woo, thou therefore hast no cause;
But rather reason thus with reason fetter:
Love sought is good, but given unsought is better.
VIOLA By innocence I swear, and by my youth,
I have one heart, one bosom, and one truth,
And that no woman has; nor never none
Shall mistress be of it, save I alone.
And so adieu, good madam; never more
Will I my master's tears to you deplore.
OLIVIA Yet come again: for thou perhaps mayst move
That heart which now abhors, to like his love.

Glossary

lowly feigning	pretending to be humble
whet	sharpen
solicit	plead for
hard construction	hard judgement
receiving	perception, intelligence
cypress	thin veil
degree	step
grise	step
vulgar proof	common experience
maugre	in spite of

All of the questions that follow relate to Act I Scene 1

A

Choose just one answer, a, b, c or d.

1 Orsino is in love with
- a) Viola
- b) Olivia
- c) Maria
- d) Curio

2 Orsino asks for
- a) food
- b) drink
- c) music
- d) his jester

3 The love that Orsino feels is
- a) unrequited
- b) courtly
- c) requited
- d) familial

4 Olivia is unhappy because
- a) her husband has died
- b) her husband has left her
- c) her brother has died
- d) she is in love with a man who doesn't love her

5 Orsino believes that
- a) Olivia will never love him
- b) Olivia will love him completely
- c) Olivia is incapable of love
- d) Olivia will love him as a brother

Score .... /5

B

Answer all parts of all questions.

1 Look at the section beginning 'O spirit of love' and ending 'Even in a minute'.
What does Orsino compare love to? Explain how this indicates Orsino's view of love.

Comparison: ....

Explanation: ....

.... 2 marks

2 Look at the section beginning 'That instant' and ending 'E're since pursue me'.
What does Orsino compare his desire to? Explain why he uses this image and what he means.

Comparison: ....

Explanation: ....

.... 3 marks

3 Look at the section beginning 'The element itself' and ending 'her sad remembrance'.
Explain exactly what Olivia has vowed to do.

....

.... 2 marks

Score .... /7

C

This is a SATs-style question. Your answer should respond to each of the bullet points.

1 **Is Orsino in love with Olivia or in love with the idea of being in love?**

You should write about:

- what he says about love
- what he says about Olivia
- the way you think he would speak and behave in this scene.

....

....
10 marks

Score .... /10

TOTAL SCORE /22

For more help on this topic see KS3 English Success Guide pages 66–75

All of the questions that follow relate to Act III Scene 1

A Choose just one answer, a, b, c or d.

1 **Olivia is in love with**
a) Orsino
b) Cesario
c) Malvolio
d) Sir Andrew

2 **When the audience know something that the characters don't, this is called**
a) irony
b) a pun
c) dramatic irony
d) doubling

3 **What did Olivia send to Viola-Cesario after their last meeting?**
a) a letter
b) flowers
c) a lock of hair
d) a ring

4 **Tyrannous means**
a) cruel
b) sensible
c) cold
d) loving

5 **Viola-Cesario is servant to**
a) Olivia
b) Orsino
c) Sir Toby
d) Sebastian

Score .... **/5**

B Answer all parts of all questions.

1 Look at the section beginning 'Have you not set'.
What image does Olivia use to describe her secret love? Find and copy three words that help to create this image.

Image: ....

Vocabulary: .... 2 marks

2 Look at the section beginning 'Stay!' and ending 'I am your fool'.
What length of words is used most here? Explain the effect of this.

Length: ....

Explanation: ....

.... 2 marks

3 In this section Viola tells Olivia 'I am not what I am'.
What does she mean and why would a Shakespearian audience find this amusing?

Meaning: ....

Explanation: ....

....

.... 3 marks

Score .... **/7**

C

This is a SATs-style question. Your answer should respond to each of the bullet points.

1 **In this scene Olivia declares her love for Cesario. Explain what you understand her opinion of love to be.**

You should write about:

- the imagery she uses
- her feelings for Cesario
- her feelings for Orsino
- the way she behaves.

....

....

....

....

....

....

....

....

....

....

....

....

....

....

....

....

....

....

....

....

....

....

....

.... 10 marks

Score .... /10

TOTAL SCORE /22

For more help on this topic see KS3 English Success Guide pages 66–75

MACBETH

Read the two extracts from the play and answer the questions that follow.

In this Scene, Macbeth tries to decide whether he should go ahead with the murder. Lady Macbeth is angry with him for being weak and persuades him to commit the murder.

ACT I SCENE 7
Macbeth's Castle near the Great Hall
Enter a butler and servants with dishes and service over the stage.
Then enter **MACBETH**

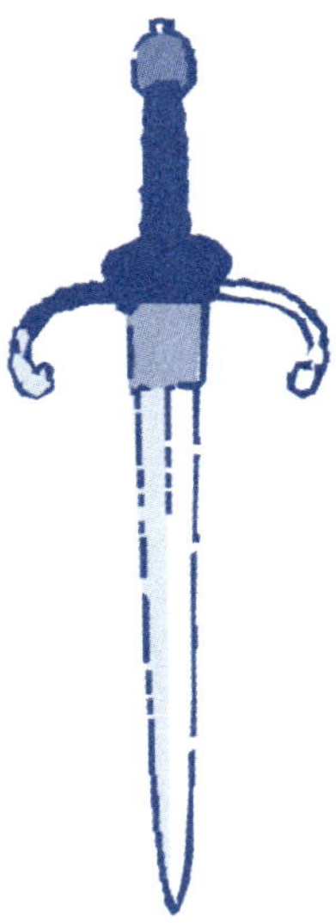

MACBETH If it were done when 'tis done, then 'twere well
It were done quickly. If th'assassination
Could trammel up the consequence and catch
With his surcease, success, that but this blow
Might be the be-all and the end-all — here,
But here, upon this bank and shoal of time,
We'd jump the life to come. But in these cases,
We still have judgement here that we but teach
Bloody instructions, which being taught, return
To plague th'inventor. This even-handed justice
Commends th'ingredients of our poison'd chalice
To our own lips. He's here in double trust:
First, as I am his kinsman and his subject,
Strong both against the deed; then, as his host,
Who should against his murderer shut the door,
Not bear the knife myself. Besides, this Duncan
Hath borne his faculties so meek, hath been
So clear in his great office, that his virtues
Will plead like angels, trumpet-tongu'd against
The deep damnation of his taking-off.
And pity, like a naked newborn babe
Striding the blast, or heaven's cherubin hors'd
Upon the sightless couriers of the air,
Shall blow the horrid deed in every eye,
That tears shall drown the wind. I have no spur
To prick the sides of my intent, but only
Vaulting ambition which o'erleaps itself
And falls on th'other – *Enter* **LADY MACBETH**
How now? What news?

LADY MACBETH He has almost supp'd. Why have you left the chamber?

MACBETH Hath he ask'd for me?

LADY MACBETH Know you not, he has?

MACBETH We will proceed no further in this business.
He hath honour'd me of late, and I have bought
Golden opinions from all sorts of people,
Which would be worn now in their newest gloss,
Not cast aside so soon.

LADY MACBETH Was the hope drunk
Wherein you dressed yourself? Hath it slept since?
And wakes it now to look so green and pale
At what it did so freely? From this time,
Such I account thy love. Art thou afeard
To be the same in thine own act and valour,
As thou art in desire? Wouldst thou have that
Which thou esteem'st the ornament of life,
And live a coward in thine own esteem,
Letting 'I dare not' wait upon 'I would',
Like the poor cat i'th'adage?

MACBETH Prithee, peace.
I dare do all that may become a man;
Who dares do more is none.

LADY MACBETH What beast was't then
That made you break this enterprise to me?
When you durst do it, then you were a man.
And to be more than what you were, you would
Be so much more the man. Nor time, nor place
Did then adhere, and yet you would make both.
They have made themselves and that their fitness now
Does unmake you. I have given suck and know
How tender 'tis to love the babe that milks me:
I would, while it was smiling in my face,
Have pluck'd my nipple from his boneless gums
And dash'd the brains out, had I so sworn
As you have done to this.

MACBETH If we should fail?

LADY MACBETH We fail?
But screw your courage to the sticking-place,
And we'll not fail. When Duncan is asleep,
Whereto the rather shall his day's hard journey
Soundly invite him, his two chamberlains
Will I with wine and wassail so convince
That memory, the warder of the brain,
Shall be a fume, and the receipt of reason
A limbeck only. When in swinish sleep
Their drenched natures lies as in a death,
What cannot you and I perform upon
Th'unguarded Duncan? What not put upon
His spongy officers, who shall bear the guilt
Of our great quell?

MACBETH Bring forth men-children only,
For thy undaunted mettle should compose
Nothing but males. Will it not be receiv'd,
When we have mark'd with blood those sleepy two
Of his own chamber and us'd their very daggers,
That they have done't?

LADY MACBETH Who dares receive it other,
As we shall make our griefs and clamour roar
Upon his death?

MACBETH I am settled and bend up
Each corporal agent to this terrible feat.
Away, and mock the time with fairest show,
False face must hide what the false heart doth know.

Glossary

trammel up	catch	**the ornament of life**	the crown
surcease	death	**break this enterprise**	share this plan
faculties	abilities as King	**wassail**	drinking toasts
sightless couriers	the wind	**each corporal agent**	every part of me

In this extract Macbeth revisits the witches after being haunted by Banquo's ghost. The witches show him several apparitions. Macbeth interprets their messages to mean that he is invincible.

ACT IV SCENE 1 lines 47 – 104
A desolate place near Forres

Enter **MACBETH**

MACBETH How now, you secret, black, and midnight hags!
What is't you do?
ALL THE WITCHES A deed without a name.
MACBETH I conjure you by that which you profess,
Howe'er you come to know it, answer me.
Though you untie the winds and let them fight
Against the churches, though the yeasty waves
Confound and swallow navigation up,
Though bladed corn be lodg'd and trees blown down,
Though castles topple on their warders' heads,
Though palaces and pyramids do slope
Their heads to their foundations, though the treasure
Of nature's germen tumble altogether
Even till destruction sicken: answer me
To what I ask you.

FIRST WITCH Speak.
SECOND WITCH Demand.
THIRD WITCH We'll answer.
FIRST WITCH Say, if thou'dst rather hear it from our mouths,
Or from our masters'?
MACBETH Call 'em, let me see 'em.
FIRST WITCH Pour in sow's blood, that hath eaten
Her nine farrow; grease that's sweaten
From the murderer's gibbet throw
Into the flame.
ALL THE WITCHES Come high or low:
Thyself and office deftly show.

Thunder. Enter **FIRST APPARITION**, *an armed Head*

MACBETH Tell me, thou unknown power —
FIRST WITCH He knows thy thought:
Hear his speech, but say thou nought.
FIRST APPARITION Macbeth, Macbeth, Macbeth: beware Macduff,
Beware the Thane of Fife. Dismiss me. Enough.
Descends

MACBETH Whate'er thou art, for thy good caution, thanks;
Thou hast harp'd my fear aright. But one word more —

FIRST WITCH He will not be commanded. Here's another,
More potent than the first.

Thunder. Enter **SECOND APPARITION,** *a bloody Child*

SECOND APPARITION Macbeth, Macbeth, Macbeth.

MACBETH Had I three ears, I'd hear thee.

SECOND APPARITION Be bloody, bold, and resolute; laugh to scorn
The power of man, for none of woman born
Shall harm Macbeth. *Descends*

MACBETH Then live, Macduff, what need I fear of thee?
But yet I'll make assurance double sure
And take a bond of fate: thou shalt not live,
That I may tell pale-hearted fear it lies,
And sleep in spite of thunder.

Thunder. Enter **THIRD APPARITION**, *a Child crowned, with a tree in his hand*

What is this,
That rises like the issue of a king
And wears upon his baby-brow the round
And top of sovereignty?

ALL THE WITCHES Listen, but speak not to't.

THIRD APPARITION Be lion-mettl'd, proud, and take no care
Who chafes, who frets, or where conspirers are.
Macbeth shall never vanquish'd be until
Great Birnam Wood to high Dunsinane hill
Shall come against him. *Descends*

MACBETH That will never be:
Who can impress the forest, bid the tree
Unfix his earthbound root? Sweet bodements, good.
Rebellious dead, rise never till the wood
Of Birnam rise, and our high-plac'd Macbeth
Shall live the lease of nature, pay his breath
To time and mortal custom. Yet my heart
Throbs to know one thing. Tell me, if your art
Can tell so much, shall Banquo's issue ever
Reign in this kingdom?

ALL THE WITCHES Seek to know no more.

MACBETH I will be satisfied. Deny me this,
And an eternal curse fall on you. Let me know.

Glossary

office	function
harped	echoed
issue	descendant
the round / And top of sovereignty	the crown
lion-mettled	courageous
impress	conscript
bodements	prophesies

All of the questions that follow relate to Act I Scene 7

A Choose just one answer, a, b, c or d.

1 **A euphemism is**
a) a joke
b) a more pleasant way of expressing something unpleasant
c) an offensive word
d) simple way of expressing a complicated idea

2 **Macbeth's best reason for killing King Duncan is**
a) his own ambition
b) Duncan is a weak king
c) Duncan is planning to have Macbeth executed
d) Duncan never promotes Macbeth

3 **When Lady Macbeth discovers that Macbeth has changed his mind about the murder, she is**
a) pleased
b) relieved
c) angry
d) afraid

4 **Who does Lady Macbeth plan to blame for the murder?**
a) Duncan's sons
b) the witches
c) Banquo
d) the guards

5 **An *adage* is**
a) a proverb
b) a joke
c) a fable
d) a lie

Score ...3... /5

B Answer all parts of all questions.

1 Find and copy two reasons given by Macbeth for not killing King Duncan and explain what each means.

Reason: ....

....

Explanation: ....

....

Reason: ....

....

Explanation: ....

.... 4 marks

2 When talking about the murder Macbeth uses many euphemisms. Find and copy two euphemisms and explain why Macbeth uses them.

Euphemisms: .... 1 mark

Explanation: ....

.... 2 marks

Score ...0... /7

C

This is a SATs-style question. Your answer should respond to each of the bullet points.

1 **Compare the thoughts and behaviour of Macbeth and Lady Macbeth in this scene.**

You should write about:

- Macbeth's thoughts about the murder when he is alone
- the way Lady Macbeth speaks to her husband
- the way the characters behave.

....

....

....

....

....

....

....

....

....

....

....

....

....

....

....

....

....

....

....

....

....

....

....

....

.... 10 marks

Score .... /10

TOTAL SCORE /22

For more help on this topic see KS3 English Success Guide pages 66–75

All of the questions that follow relate to Act IV Scene I

A Choose just one answer, a, b, c or d.

1 Macbeth learns his future from
a) the witches
b) Hecate
c) three apparitions
d) looking into the cauldron

2 The first apparition tells Macbeth to
a) kill Macduff
b) fear Macduff
c) save Macduff
d) join forces with Macduff

3 The second apparition tells Macbeth
a) he will never be killed
b) he cannot be hurt by a man
c) a woman will kill him
d) he cannot be harmed by a man born of a woman

4 Macbeth wants to know
a) if Duncan's son will be king
b) if Banquo's descendants will be kings
c) if Macduff will be king
d) if Macduff's son will be king

5 In this scene the witches and the apparitions usually speak in
a) blank verse
b) rhyming couplets
c) rhyming triplets
d) trochaic pentameter

Score 3 /5

B Answer all parts of all questions.

1 Macbeth demands to know his future irrespective of the consequences. Look at the section beginning 'I conjure you' and ending 'Even till destruction sicken'.
Explain two possible consequences that Macbeth mentions.

....

....

.... 2 marks

2 In this scene Macbeth's language becomes more and more like the witches. **Explain how Shakespeare makes Macbeth sound more like the witches.**

....

....

....

.... 3 marks

3 **Explain how Macbeth interprets the third apparition.**

....

....

.... 2 marks

Score ...... /7

C This is a SATs-style question. Your answer should respond to each of the bullet points.

1 How does Shakespeare create a mood of tension and horror in this scene?

You should write about:

- what the witches say
- the way Macbeth speaks and behaves
- the presentation of the apparitions.

10 marks

Score .... /10

TOTAL SCORE /22

For more help on this topic see KS3 English Success Guide pages 68–75

HENRY V

Read the two extracts from the play and answer the questions that follow.

In this scene, King Henry, having discovered the traitors' plot, confronts and reproaches them for betraying his trust.

ACT II SCENE 2 lines 91 – end

KING But oh, What shall I say to thee, Lord Scroop, thou cruel,
Ingrateful, savage and inhuman creature?
Thou that didst bear the key of all my counsels,
That knew'st the very bottom of my soul,
That almost mightst have coined me into gold,
Wouldst thou have practis'd on me for thy use?
May it be possible that foreign hire
Could out of thee extract one spark of evil
That might annoy my finger? 'Tis so strange
That though the truth of it stands off as gross
As black on white my eye will scarcely see it.
Treason and murder ever kept together,
As two yoke-devils sworn to either's purpose
Working so grossly in a natural cause
That admiration did not whoop at them.
But thou 'gainst all proportion didst bring in
Wonder to wait on treason and on murder,
And whatsoever cunning fiend it was
That wrought upon thee so preposterously
Hath got the voice in hell for excellence.
All other devils that suggest by treasons
Do botch and bungle up damnation
With patches, colours, and with forms being fetch'd
From glistering semblances of piety;
But he that temper'd thee bade thee stand up,
Gave thee no instance why thou shouldst do treason,
Unless to dub thee with the name of traitor.
If that same demon that hath gull'd thee thus
Should with his lion gait walk the whole world
He might return to vasty Tartar back
And tell the legions 'I can never win
A soul so easy as that Englishman's.'
Oh, how hast thou with jealousy infected
The sweetness of affiance? Show men dutiful?
Why, so didst thou. Seem they grave and learned?
Why, so didst thou. Come they of noble family?
Why, so didst thou. Seem they religious?

Why, so didst thou. Or are they spare in diet,
Free from gross passion, or of mirth or anger,
Constant in spirit, not swerving with the blood,
Garnish'd and deck'd in modest complement,
Not working with the eye without the ear,
And but in purged judgement trusting neither?
Such and so finely bolted didst thou seem.
And thus thy fall hath left a kind of blot
To mark the full fraught man, and best endow'd
With some suspicion. I will weep for thee,
For this revolt of thine, methinks, is like
Another fall of man. Their faults are open.
Arrest them to the answer of the law,
And God acquit them of their practices.

EXETER I arrest thee of high treason, by the name of Richard Earl of Cambridge. I arrest thee of high treason, by the name of Henry, Lord Scroop of Masham. I arrest thee of high treason, by the name of Thomas Gray, knight of Northumberland.

SCROOP Our purposes God justly hath discover'd,
And I repent my fault more than my death,
Which I beseech your highness to forgive,
Although my body pay the price of it.

CAMBRIDGE For me, the gold of France did not seduce
Although I did admit it as a motive
The sooner to effect what I intended.
But God be thanked for prevention,
Which I in sufferance heartily will rejoice,
Beseeching God and you to pardon me.

GRAY Never did faithful subject more rejoice
At the discovery of most dangerous treason
Than I do at this hour joy o'er myself,
Prevented from a damned enterprise.
My fault, but not my body, pardon, sovereign.

KING God quit you in His mercy. Hear your sentence.
You have conspir'd against our royal person,
Join'd with an enemy proclaim'd, and from his coffers
Receiv'd the golden earnest of our death;
Wherein you would have sold your king to slaughter,
His princes and his peers to servitude,
His subjects to oppression and contempt,
And his whole kingdom into desolation.
Touching our person seek we no revenge,
But we our kingdom's safety must so tender,
Whose ruin you have sought, that to her laws
We do deliver you. Get you therefore hence,
Poor miserable wretches, to your death,
The taste whereof God of His mercy give
You patience to endure, and true repentance
Of all your dear offences. Bear them hence.

Exeunt CAMBRIDGE, SCROOP, GRAY *and* OFFICERS

Now lords, for France, the enterprise whereof
Shall be to you as us, like glorious.
We doubt not of a fair and lucky war,
Since God so graciously hath brought to light
This dangerous treason lurking in our way
To hinder our beginnings. We doubt not now
But every rub is smoothed on our way.
Then forth, dear countrymen. Let us deliver
Our puissance into the hand of God,
Putting it straight in expedition.
Cheerly to sea, the signs of war advance.
No king of England if not king of France! *Flourish. Exeunt*

GLOSSARY

Hire	bribery
Gull'd	deceived
Affiance	trust
Puissance	power, forces

In this extract the King urges his troops on to make one last assault on Harfleur.

ACT III SCENE 1 (complete scene) and SCENE 2 lines 1–23

Enter KING, EXETER, BEDFORD, *and* GLOUCESTER. *Enter* soldiers *with scaling ladders at Harfleur*

KING Once more unto the breach, dear friends, once more,
Or close the wall up with our English dead!
In peace there's nothing so becomes a man
As modest stillness and humility.
But when the blast of war blows in our ears,
Then imitate the action of the tiger:
Stiffen the sinews, conjure up the blood,
Disguise fair nature with hard-favour'd rage.
Then lend the eye a terrible aspect,
Let it pry through the portage of the head,
Like the brass cannon. Let the brow o'erwhelm it
As fearfully as doth a galled rock
O'erhang and jutty his confounded base,
Swill'd with the wild and wasteful ocean.
Now set the teeth and stretch the nostril wide,
Hold hard the breath, and bend up every spirit
To his full height. On, on, you noble English,
Whose blood is fet from fathers of war-proof,
Fathers that like so many Alexanders
Have in these parts from morn till even fought,
And sheath'd their swords for lack of argument.
Dishonour not your mothers. Now attest
That those whom you call'd fathers did beget you.
Be copy now to men of grosser blood,
And teach them how to war. And you, good yeomen,
Whose limbs were made in England, show us here

The mettle of your pasture. Let us swear
That you are worth your breeding, which I doubt not,
For there is none of you so mean and base
That hath not noble lustre in your eyes.
I see you stand like greyhounds in the slips,
Straining upon the start. The game's afoot.
Follow your spirit, and upon this charge
Cry 'God for Harry, England, and Saint George!'

Alarm, and chambers go off. Exeunt

GLOSSARY

Hard-favour'd	grim featured
Aspect	expression
Fet	inherited
Alexander	Alexander the Great
Copy	example
Slips	leashes

SCENE 2

Enter NYM, BARDOLPH, PISTOL, *and* BOY

BARDOLPH On, on, on, on, on, to the breach, to the breach!

NYM Pray thee, corporal, stay. The knocks are too hot, and for mine own part I have not a case of lives. The humour of it is too hot, that is the very plain-song of it.

PISTOL 'The plain-song' is most just, for humours do abound. Knocks go and come, God's vassals drop and die,

[Sings] And sword and shield,
In bloody field,
Doth win immortal fame.

BOY Would I were in an ale-house in London. I would give all my fame for a pot of ale, and safety.

PISTOL And I.

[Sings] If wishes would prevail with me,
My purpose should not fail with me,
But thither would I hie.

BOY *[Sings]* As duly
But not as truly
As bird doth sing on bough.

Enter LLEWELLYN

LLEWELLYN Up to the preach, you dogs! Avaunt, you cullions!

PISTOL Be merciful, great duke, to men of mould! Abate thy rage, abate thy manly rage! Abate thy rage, great duke! Good bawcock, bate thy rage. Use lenity, sweet chuck.

NYM These be good humours! Your honour wins bad humours!

Exeunt PISTOL, BARDOLPH, *and* NYM, *pursued by* LLEWELLYN

All of the questions that follow relate to Act II Scene 2

A Choose just one answer, a, b, c or d.

1 **Which of the following characters is not a traitor?**
a) Scroop
b) Exeter
c) Cambridge
d) Gray

2 **Who has upset the King the most?**
a) Scroop
b) Exeter
c) Cambridge
d) Gray

3 **What reason does Henry give for executing the traitors?**
a) he is upset that they were trying to kill him
b) God has told him to do it
c) he wants to make an example of them
d) he wants to protect his kingdom

4 **Henry wants to be**
a) King of England
b) King of Spain
c) King of Bavaria
d) King of France

5 **Henry thinks that the discovery of the plot is**
a) a sign that they will be unlucky in the coming war
b) a sign that they will be successful in the coming war
c) God's way of punishing the king
d) the first of many problems that they will have to face

Score .... /5

B Answer all parts of all questions.

1 Look at what Henry says to Lord Scroop, lines 91–92: 'What shall I say to thee'. **What is the effect of using the adjectives *cruel, ingrateful, savage* and *inhuman*?**

.... 1 mark

2 Look at the section beginning 'Oh, how hast thou' and ending 'Or are they spare in diet' (lines 123–128). **What devices does Shakespeare use in this section and what effect do they have?**

Device: ....

Effect: ....

....

Device: ....

Effect: ....

.... 4 marks

3 Henry describes Scroop's betrayal as 'like another fall of man'. **What does he mean and how does this reveal how upset he feels?**

Meaning: ....

Explanation: .... 2 marks

Score .... /7

C

This is a SATs-style question. Your answer should respond to each of the bullet points.

1 How does Shakespeare reveal Henry's character and changing emotions in this scene?

You should write about:

- the way Henry speaks to Scroop
- the range of emotions that Henry displays
- his reasons for executing the traitors
- his behaviour towards the end of the scene.

....

....

....

....

....

....

....

....

....

....

....

....

....

....

....

....

....

....

....

....

....

....

....

.... 10 marks

Score .... /10

TOTAL SCORE /22

For more help on this topic see KS3 English Success Guide pages 66–75

All of the questions that follow relate to Act III Scene 1 and 2

A Choose just one answer, a, b, c or d.

1 **Henry wants his troops to**
a) attack for the first time
b) retreat
c) attack again
d) break through the wall

2 **According to Henry, which of the following qualities are desirable in war?**
a) modesty
b) stillness
c) rage
d) humility

3 **Yeomen are**
a) foot soldiers
b) from the cities
c) old soldiers
d) stable hands

4 **Henry compares his troops to**
a) greyhounds
b) wolves
c) puppies
d) lions

5 **Nym and Pistol are**
a) anxious to fight
b) wishing they were in an ale house
c) fighting with each other
d) waiting for further orders

Score .... /5

B Answer all parts of all questions.

1 Why does Henry refer to the soldiers as 'dear friends'?

.... 1 mark

2 Find and copy an example of an imperative command and explain why it is used.

Example: ....

Explanation: .... 2 marks

3 Look at the section beginning 'Whose blood is fet' and ending 'which I doubt not'. The part of the speech is full of references to family and breeding. Explain why these references are used.

....

....

.... 2 marks

4 Find and copy an example of a simile in Henry's speech and explain why it is used.

Simile: ....

Explanation: ....

.... 2 marks

Score .... /7

C These are SATs-style questions. Your answers should respond to each of the bullet points.

1 Explain how Shakespeare uses language in Henry's speech to inspire the troops.

You should write about:

- the imagery he uses
- his references to blood and inheritance
- the way he includes all of the troops.

....

....

....

....

....

....

....

....

....

....

....

....

.... 6 marks

2 Explain the effect of continuing the play with a scene featuring Nym, Bardolph and Pistol.

....

....

....

....

....

....

....

....

....

....

.... 4 marks

Score .... **/10**

TOTAL SCORE /22

For more help on this topic see KS3 English Success Guide pages 66–75

SPELLING

A Choose just one answer, A, B, C or D.

1 **A word which sounds the same as another word but is spelt differently and has a different meaning is a**
a) homograph
b) homonym
c) homophone
d) synonym

2 **Words ending in *ch* are pluralized by adding**
a) s b) 's c) ies d) es

3 **The correct spelling meaning *belonging to it* is**
a) it's b) its c) its' d) it is

4 ***ies* is the correct plural ending of**
a) all words ending in y
b) words ending in a *vowel* then y
c) words ending in a *consonant* then y
d) words ending in *f*

5 **A group of letters added to the beginning of a word to change the meaning is**
a) a suffix
b) a prefix
c) a synonym
d) an antonym

Score .... /5

B Answer all parts of all questions.

1 The following words are all spelt incorrectly. Write the correct spelling next to each one.

acommodation ....   churche's (plural) ....
comited ....   leafs ....
strawberrys ....   possable ....
seperate ....   sucessfull ....
definate...........................   beautyful .... 10 marks

2 Pluralise the following words.

Monkey   boy   factory   baby   try

....

....

.... 2 marks

3 Write the rule for pluralising words ending in y.

.... 1 mark

Score .... /13

C Answer all parts of all questions.

1 There are seven spelling mistakes in the passage below. Find each mistake and write the correct spellings beneath.

He undressed quickley, bending his pumps free of his heels and sliding them off without untying the laces. When he stood up the black soles of his sockes stamped damp imprints on the dry floor, witch developed into a haphazard set of footprints when he removed his socks and steped around pulling his jeans down. His ankels and knees were ingrained with ancient dirt which seemed to belong to the pigmentasion of his skin. His left leg sported a mud stripe, and both his knees were encrusted. The surfaces of these mobile crusts where hair-lined, and with every flexion of the knee these lines opened into frown-like furrows.

from *A Kestrel for a Knave*
by Barry Hines

1 ....

2 ....

3 ....

4 ....

5 ....

6 ....

7 .... 7 marks

2 Choose the correct homophone for each sentence that follows.

The books are on the table over **their / they're / there.**

Read **threw / through** your answers before you finish the exam.

Were / We're going on holiday next week.

I cut myself with the **sore / saw** and now my arm is really **sore / saw**.

I don't **no / know** what the answer is.

Did you **hear / here** that noise?

The **not / knot** is too tight.

7 marks

Score .... /14

PUNCTUATION AND GRAMMAR

A

Choose just one answer, a, b, c or d.

1 A simple sentence does not contain
a) a main clause
b) a comma
c) a verb
d) a subordinate clause

2 A sentence joining two main clauses with *and* is
a) a simple sentence
b) a compound sentence
c) a complex sentence
d) a concrete sentence

3 Which of the following cannot be used to end a sentence?
a) full stop b) question mark
c) comma d) exclamation mark

4 Which of the following statements is incorrect?
a) a sentence usually contains a verb
b) a sentence must begin with a capital letter
c) never begin a sentence with the word *because*
d) sentences don't always end with a full stop

5 An embedded clause
a) splits a main clause
b) ends a sentence
c) is always a main clause
d) must contain a non-finite verb

Score .... /5

B

Answer all parts of all questions.

1 Change these two sentences into one compound sentence.
I went to the shop. I bought a chocolate bar.

.... 1 mark

2 Move the subordinate clause in the following sentence, changing the punctuation if necessary.
The trains were late due to track repairs.

.... 2 marks

3 Embed the subordinate clause in the following sentence, changing the punctuation if necessary.
Filled with despair, the teacher marked the exam papers.

.... 2 marks

4 Add apostrophes to the following.

dont	whos (who is)	couldnt	doesnt
Joannes bag	the girls (plural) bags	the girls (singular) bag	the poets writing

8 marks

Score .... /13

C Answer all parts of all questions.

1a Give three reasons for beginning a new paragraph.

1 ....

2 ....

3 ....

1b This extract was originally written in three paragraphs. Identify where each new paragraph should begin and end.

I took a train to Liverpool. They were having a festival of litter when I arrived. Citizens had taken time off from their busy activities to add crisp packets, empty cigarette boxes, and carrier-bags to the otherwise bland and neglected landscape. They fluttered gaily in the bushes and brought colour and texture to pavements and gutters. And to think that elsewhere we stick these objects in rubbish bags. In another bout of extravagant madness, I had booked a room in the Adelphi Hotel. I had seen it from the street on earlier visits and it appeared to have an old-fashioned grandeur about it that I was keen to investigate. On the other hand, it looked expensive and I wasn't sure my trousers could stand another session in the trouser press. So I was most agreeably surprised when I checked in to discover that I was entitled to a special weekend rate and that there would be money spare for a nice meal and a parade of beer in any of the many wonderful pubs in which Liverpool specializes. And so, soon afterwards, I found myself, like all fresh arrivals in Liverpool, in the grand and splendorous surroundings of the Philharmonic, clutching a pint glass…

from *Notes from a Small Island*
by Bill Bryson

1 ....

2 ....

3 .... 6 marks

2 Add the correct punctuation to the following sentences.

a) when the rope snapped the climber who was very frightened fell and broke his leg

....

b) can I go out tonight mum asked Alison

....

c) when the alarm rang the workers left the building calmly

....

d) gosh exclaimed the woman I didn't see you there

.... 8 marks

Score .... /14

TOTAL SCORE /32

For more help on this topic see KS3 English Success Guide pages 88–93

SATS EXAM PRACTICE

Paper One
Reading and Writing

Reading

- The reading task is one hour plus 15 minutes reading time.
- Read the three texts provided and answer all the questions that follow.
- Answer each question in the space provided.
- The number of marks available for each task is printed next to the question.

Writing

- The writing task is 45 minutes long. This includes time for planning.
- Complete your planning in the space provided. Write your answer on a separate sheet of paper.
- The number of marks available for each skill tested is printed beneath the question.

Reading

Read the three texts that follow and answer all of the questions in the reading section.

Text 1 – Fiction

In this extract, Billy Casper continues his routine to tame and train the kestrel he found when he went nesting.

Billy approached the hawk slowly, regarding it obliquely, ducking and chanting softly, 'Kes Kes Kes'. The hawk bobbed her head and shifted along the perch. Billy held out his gauntlet and offered her a scrap of beef. She reached forward and grasped it with her beak, and tried to pull it from his glove. Billy gripped the beef tightly between forefinger and thumb; and in order to obtain more leverage, the hawk stepped on to his fist. He allowed her to take the beef, then replaced her on the perch, touching the backs of her legs against the wood so that she stepped backwards on to it. He dipped into the leather satchel at his hip and offered her a fresh scrap; this time holding it just out of range of her reaching beak. She bobbed her head and tippled forward slightly, regained balance, then glanced about, uncertain, like someone up on the top board for the first time.

'Come on, Kes. Come on then.'

He stood still. The hawk looked at the meat, then jumped on to the glove and took it. Billy smiled and replaced it with a tough strip of beef, and as the hawk busied herself with it, he attached a swivel to the ends of the jesses dangling from her legs, slipped the jesses between the first and second fingers of his glove, and felt into his bag for the leash. The hawk looked up from her feeding. Billy rubbed his finger and thumb to make the meat move between them, and as the hawk attended to it again, he threaded the leash through the lower ring of the swivel and pulled it all the way through until the knot at the other end snagged on the ring. He completed the security by looping the leash twice round his glove and tying the end round his little finger.

He walked to the door and slowly pushed it open. The hawk looked up, and as he moved out into the full light, her eyes seemed to expand, her body contract as she flattened her feathers. She bobbed her head, once, twice, then bated, throwing herself sideways off his glove and hanging upside down, thrashing her wings and screaming. Billy waited for her to stop, then placed his hand gently under her breast and lifted her back on to the glove. She bated again; and again, and each time Billy lifted her carefully back up, until finally she stayed up, beak half open, panting, glaring round.

'What's up then? What's a matter with you, Kes? Anybody'd think you'd never been out before.'

The hawk roused her feathers and bent to her meat, her misdemeanours apparently forgotten.

Billy walked her round the garden, speaking quietly to her all the time. Then he turned up the path at the side of the house and approached the front gate, watching the hawk for her actions. A car approached. The hawk tensed, watched it then resumed her meal as it sped away up the avenue. On the opposite pavement a little boy, pedalling a tricycle round in tight circles, looked up and saw them, immediately unwound and drove straight off the pavement, making the tin mudguards clank as the wheels jonked down into the gutter. Billy held the hawk away from him, anticipating a bate, but she glanced up at the sound, or at the boy as he cycled towards them and hutched his tricycle up on the pavement.

'Oo that's a smasher. What is it?'

'What tha think it is?'

'Is it an owl?'

'It's a kestrel.'

'Where you got it from?'

'Found it.'
'Is it tame?'
'It's trained. I've trained it.'
Billy pointed to himself, and smiled across at the hawk.
'Don't it look fierce?'
'It is.'
'Does it kill things and eat 'em?'
'Course it does. It kills little kids on bikes.'
The boy laughed without smiling.
'It don't.'
'What's tha think that it's eating now then?'
'It's only a piece of meat.'
'It's a piece o' leg off a kid it caught yesterday. When it catches 'em it sits on their handlebars and rips 'em to pieces. Eyes first.'

The boy looked down at the chrome handlebars and began to swing them from side to side, making the front wheel describe a steady arc like a windscreen wiper.

'I bet I dare stroke it.'
'Tha'd better not.'
'I'll bet I dare.'
'It'll have thi hand off if tha tries.'

The boy stood up, straddling the tricycle frame, and slowly lifted one hand towards the hawk. She mantled her wings over the meat, then struck out with her scaly yellow legs, screaming and raking at the hand with her talons. The boy jerked his arm back with such force that its momentum carried his whole body over the tricycle and on to the ground. He scrambled up, as wide-eyed as the hawk, mounted and pedalled off down the pavement, his legs whirring like bee's wings.

from *A Kestrel for a Knave*
by Barry Hines

Text 2 – Non-Fiction

In this extract Douglas Adams describes his experience of scuba diving in Australia, looking for giant manta rays.

For the afternoon dive, Ian said he wanted to take me in a different direction from the boat. I asked him why, and he looked non-committal. I followed him down into the water and slowly we flippered our way across to a new part of the reef. When we reached it, the flat top of the reef was about four feet below the surface, and the sunlight dappled gently over the extraordinary shapes and colours of the brain coral, the antler coral, the sea ferns and anemones. The stuff you see beneath the water often seems like a wild parody of the stuff you see above it. I remember the thought I had when first I dived on the Barrier Reef years ago, which was that this was all the stuff that people used to have on their mantelpieces in the fifties. It took me a while to rid myself of the notion that the reef was a load of kitsch.

I've never learnt the names of a lot of fish. I always swot them up on the boat and forget them a week later. But watching the breathtaking variety of shape and movement keeps me entranced for hours, or would if the oxygen allowed. If I were not an atheist, I think I would have to be a Catholic because if it wasn't the forces of natural selection that designed fish, it must have been an Italian.

I was moving forward slowly in the shallows. A few feet in front of me the reef gradually dipped down into a broad valley. The valley floor was wide and dark and flat. Ian was directing my attention toward it. I didn't know why. There seemed to be just an absence of interesting coral. And then, as I looked, the whole black floor of the valley slowly lifted upward and started gently to waft its way away from us. As it moved, its edges were rippling softly and I could see that underneath it was pure white. I was transfixed by the realisation that what I was looking at was an eight-foot-wide giant manta ray.

It banked away in a wide, sweeping turn in the deeper water. It seemed to be moving breathtakingly slowly, and I was desperate to keep up with it. I came down the side of the reef to follow it. Ian motioned me not to alarm the creature, but just move slowly. I had quickly realised that its size was deceptive and it was moving much more swiftly than I realised. It banked again round the contour of the reef, and I began to see its shape more clearly. It was very roughly diamond-shaped. Its tail is not long, like a sting ray's. The most extraordinary thing is its head. Where you would expect its head to be, it's almost as if something has taken a bite out of it instead. From the two forward points – the outer edges of the 'bite', if you see what I mean – depend two horns, folded downward. And on each of these horns is a single large black eye.

As it moved, shimmering and undulating its giant wings, folding itself through the water, I felt that I was looking at the single most beautiful and unearthly thing I had ever seen in my life. Some people have described them as looking like living stealth bombers, but it is an evil image to apply to a creature so majestic, fluid, and benign.

I followed it as it swam around the outside of the reef. I couldn't follow fast or well, but it was making such wide, sweeping turns that I only had to move relatively short distances round the reef to keep it in sight. Twice, even three times it circled round the reef and then at last it disappeared and I thought I had lost it for good. I stopped and looked around. No. It had definitely gone. I was saddened, but exhilarated with wonder at what I had seen. Then I became aware of a shadow moving on the sea floor at the periphery of my vision. I looked up, unprepared for what I then saw.

The manta ray soared over the top of the reef above me, only this time it had two more in its wake behind it. Together the three vast creatures, moving in perfect, undulating harmony of line, as if following invisible rollercoaster rails, sped off and away till they were lost at last in the darkening distance of the water.

I was very quiet that evening as we packed the Sub Bug back into its big silver box. I thanked Ian for finding the manta rays. I said I understood about not riding them.

'Ah, no worries, mate,' he said. 'No worries at all.'

from *The Salmon of Doubt*
by Douglas Adams

Text 3 – Media Text

Mickey was bundled into the back of a car. After several miles, his owner pulled up, opened the door, and flung Mickey out onto the road.

Mickey was just inches away from being crushed to death when he was rescued and taken to safety.

This case is not unusual. Every year people who are bored with their new pets simply throw them away.

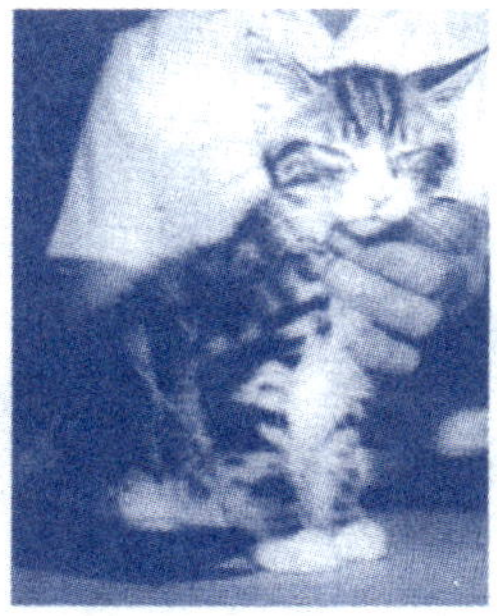

This kitten was barely recognisable after avoiding a horrifying death. Some youths tried to drown her in engine oil. We named her Olive.

Remarkably, despite her suffering, Olive made a good recovery, and now has a safe new home. The Inspector who found her says "Olive's story shows the senseless cruelty the Society has to deal with on a daily basis".

Just a small regular gift of £3 a month can help our work to prevent animals suffering cruelty

Whether at local, national or international level, the RSPCA campaigns for improvements in animal welfare.

We are currently concerned with an early phasing out of the battery cage, a ban on hunting with dogs, improved conditions for farm, zoo and circus animals and finding humane alternatives to replace animals in experiments.

Members of the public can use the RSPCA's National Cruelty Line to report animals in need of our help.

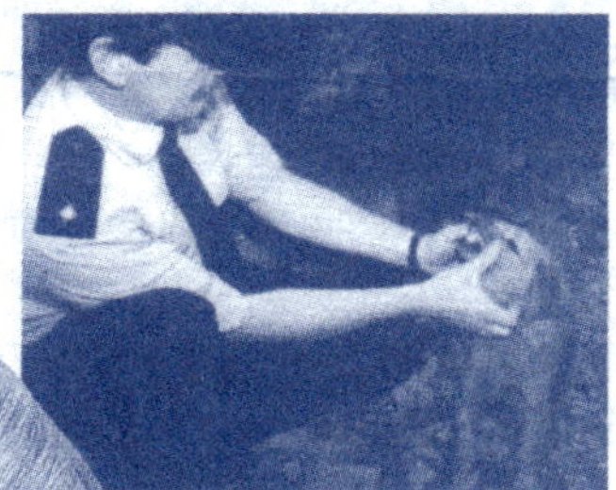

Keeping a watchful eye: Alan Pugh an RSPCA Market Inspector. A recent RSPCA survey of animal welfare at livestock markets in England and Wales revealed that many were failing to comply with basic welfare rules.

The vital RSPCA National Cruelty Line – 08705 555 999 – was set up over two years ago. This emergency service is being used on average every 20 seconds of the day by someone concerned about an animal in need of our help.

RSPCA

The RSPCA runs 4 hospitals, 51 animal centres, 39 clinics and a further 19 animal welfare centres in England and Wales. In 1998 an astonishing total of 286,540 treatments were given.

An orphaned baby hare is fed using a syringe in one of the RSPCA's animal hospitals.

RSPCA Inspectors respond quickly to reports of cruelty to animals, acting to prevent ill-treatment. Our 320 RSPCA Inspectors form the largest non-governmental law enforcement agency in the UK – in 1998 investigating 124,374 complaints.

RSPCA Inspectors – the front line against cruelty to animals.

Registered charity no. 219099

The aims of the RSPCA are to prevent cruelty and promote kindness to animals. Your donation will contribute to this important work.

Reading Test

You have 1 hour to complete this test. Answer all of the questions.

The spaces for each answer and the number of marks indicate how much you need to write.

Questions 1–6 are about *A Kestrel for a Knave.*

1 Complete the following table, giving one thing that Billy does with each item.

Item	What Billy does
scrap of beef	
swivel	
leash	

1 mark

2 What does the hawk do when it bates? Tick one box.

Fly away ☐

Hang upside down from the glove ☐

Eat a scrap of meat ☐

Freeze and remain silent ☐

1 mark

3 Look at the section 'Billy approached the hawk slowly' to 'tying the end round his little finger'.

From this section how do you know that Billy knows a lot about how to deal with the hawk? Give **two** examples of what he says or does and explain how this shows he is very knowledgeable.

Example: ....

Explanation: ....

....

....

Example: ....

Explanation: ....

....

.... 4 marks

4 Look at the conversation between Billy and the boy on the tricycle. Why does the boy 'laugh without smiling'?

....

....

....

....

.... 2 marks

5 Look at the final paragraph beginning 'The boy stood up, straddling the tricycle frame'.

How does the writer create a sense of the boy's fear in this paragraph?

You should write about:

- the way the hawk is described
- the language used to describe the boy's actions.

....

....

....

....

....

....

....

....

....

....

....

....

.... 5 marks

6 How does the writer create the sense that Billy is at ease with the wild bird he is training?

You should write about:

- the way Billy behaves towards the hawk
- the way the hawk responds to Billy
- the difference between the hawk's behaviour with Billy and with the boy on the tricycle.

....

....

....

....

....

....

....

....

....

....

....

....

....

....

....

....

....

....

....

.... 6 marks

Questions 7–12 are about *The Salmon of Doubt*

7 Look at the paragraph beginning 'I was moving forward slowly'.

How does the writer create a feeling of slow, gentle movement? Give one example and explain what effect it has.

Example: ....

....

Explanation: ....

.... 2 marks

8 What does the phrase 'I was transfixed by the realisation' suggest about how the writer felt about seeing a manta ray?

....

....

....

.... 2 marks

9 Look at the paragraph beginning 'As it moved'. Give two examples from the paragraph that show how the writer feels about the manta ray and explain why each is effective.

Example: ....

....

Explanation: ....

....

....

....

Example: ....

....

Explanation: ....

....

....

.... 4 marks

10 Look at the section 'No. It had definitely gone' to 'distance of the water'.

Why does the writer feel 'saddened but exhilarated'?

....

....

.... 2 marks

11 How does the writer create a feeling of excitement and surprise in this section?

....

....

....

....

....

....

....

.... 4 marks

12 How successful is the writer in recreating his underwater experience?

You should write about:

- how he sets the scene
- his description of the manta ray
- the way he involves the reader.

....

....

....

....

....

....

....

....

....

.... 5 marks

Questions 13–16 are about the RSPCA leaflet

13 What is the purpose of this leaflet? Give two ways you can tell this is the purpose.

Purpose: ....

....

....

1 ....

....

2 ....

.... 3 marks

14 Why are inverted commas placed around the words 'Olive's story . . . a daily basis'?

....

....

.... 1 mark

What is the effect of including this text?

....

....

.... 1 mark

15 Look at the banner heading. Comment on the use of the words 'just', 'small' and 'prevent animals suffering cruelty' in the heading.

....

....

....

....

....

.... 2 marks

16 Comment on the overall effectiveness of the layout of the leaflet.

You should write about:

- use of pictures
- font size and style
- general organisation.

.... 5 marks

End of test

Writing

You have 45 minutes to complete this test. You should spend 5–10 minutes planning your writing.

Complete your plan in the space below. Write your answer on a separate sheet of paper.

This task is worth 30 marks. You will be awarded marks for:

- **Sentence structure and punctuation (5 marks)**
- **Paragraph organisation and textual cohesion (5 marks)**
- **Composition and effect (15 marks)**
- **Spelling (5 marks)**

1 Imagine that you do some volunteer work for a local animal sanctuary which takes in stray and neglected pets as well as caring for injured wild animals and birds. The animal sanctuary will have to close in three months time unless extra funding can be raised.

Write a letter to your local council to persuade them to give a grant to the animal sanctuary.

Make your writing as persuasive as possible but remember it is a formal letter.

Planning sheet

Make brief notes under the followings headings:

Services provided by the animal sanctuary

....

....

What the money is needed for

....

....

Benefits to the council and local community

....

....

Word bank

List any persuasive/emotive words or phrases you might use in your letter.

....

....

EDUCATIONAL

SATS EXAM PRACTICE

Paper Two
Shakespeare Reading and Writing

Reading

- The reading task is based on the detailed study of two scenes from one of three Shakespeare plays.
- The reading task is 45 minutes long.
- Answer one question on the play that you have studied (*Twelfth Night, Macbeth* or *Henry V*).
- Write your answer on a separate sheet of paper.

Writing

- The writing task is related to ideas or themes contained in the Shakespeare plays.
- The task is 30 minutes long. This includes time for planning.
- Complete your planning in the space provided. Write your answer on a separate sheet of paper.
- The number of marks available for each skill tested is printed beneath the question.

Reading

Find the extracts from the play you have studied.

Twelfth Night **pages 52–55**
Macbeth **pages 60–63**
Henry V **pages 68–71**

There is one question on each play. Answer the question about the play you have studied. You have 45 minutes to complete this task. There are 30 marks available for this task.

1 ***Twelfth Night*: Act 1 Scene 1 and Act 3 Scene 1 line 78–end**
In these scenes Orsino and Olivia declare their love for characters they do not know well and who do not return their love. They could both be described as being more in love with the idea of love than anything else.

How does Shakespeare use these characters to explore the idea of unrequited love?

You should write about:

- the language they use to describe their feelings
- the way their feelings make them behave
- how the audience responds to these characters
- whether you think they are really in love or not.

2 ***Macbeth*: Act 1 Scene 7 and Act 4 Scene 1 lines 47–104**
In both of these scenes Macbeth is greatly influenced by his wife and then the witches.

How much influence do the female characters have over Macbeth's thoughts and actions?

You should write about:

- what Macbeth says when he is alone on stage
- how Lady Macbeth persuades Macbeth to go ahead with the murder
- the way that Macbeth interprets the apparitions
- who you feel is most responsible for Macbeth's actions.

3 ***Henry V*: Act 2 Scene 2 line 76 – end and Act 3 Scene 1 (complete scene) and Scene 2 lines 1–27**
It is clear that King Henry V is by far the most important character in the play and often the most important thing that other characters do is reveal another aspect of the King's character.

How does Shakespeare reveal the depth of Henry V's character in these scenes?

You should write about:

- the way he deals with the traitors
- what he says to Scroop
- the way he rallies his troops
- what the behaviour of other characters reveals about the King.

Writing

You have 30 minutes to complete this task. You should spend 5–10 minutes planning your writing.

Complete your plan in the space below. Write your answer on a separate sheet of paper.

This task is worth 20 marks. You will be awarded marks for:

- **Vocabulary (4 marks)**
- **Sentence structure/punctuation and paragraph organisation (8 marks)**
- **Composition and effect (8 marks).**

In *Macbeth*, Shakespeare explores how the main character's life is completely changed by his ambition.

Write three paragraphs about one of your own ambitions.

You should write to:

- **inform** the reader what your ambition is
- **explain** how you hope to achieve your ambition
- **describe** how you would feel if you achieved your ambition.

Planning sheet

Make brief notes under the followings headings:

Ambition

....

....

....

....

How to achieve ambition

....

....

....

....

Feelings

....

....

....

....

End of test